THE LEGAL SPLIT IN
CHILD PROTECTION

Essays on Law, Policy and Psychiatry
Peter Fritz Walter

Codependence
Coping with Addiction, Sadism and Abuse

Eight Dynamic Patterns of Living
Base Elements of True Civilization

Emotional Flow
A Holistic Approach to Healing Sadism

Love or Laws?
When Law Punishes Life

Minotaur Unveiled
A Historical Assessment of Adult-Child Sexual Interaction

Natural Order
Thesis, Antithesis and Synthesis in Human Evolution

Pedophilia Revisited
The Making of a Crime for Justifying Lacking Social Policy

The Commercial Exploitation of Abuse
A Study on Social Policy

The Legal Split in Child Protection
Overcoming the Double Standard

The Roots of Violence
Why Humans Are Not by Nature Violent

THE LEGAL SPLIT IN CHILD PROTECTION

Overcoming the Double Standard

Peter Fritz Walter

Published by Sirius-C Media Galaxy LLC

Business Filings Incorporated

108 West 13th St., Wilmington, DE 19801, USA

©2018 Peter Fritz Walter. Some rights reserved.

Essays on Law, Policy and Psychiatry, Vol. 9

Creative Commons Attribution 4.0 International License

This publication may be distributed, used for an adaptation or for derivative works, also for commercial purposes, as long as the rights of the author are attributed. The attribution must be given to the best of the user's ability with the information available. Third party licenses or copyright of quoted resources are untouched by this license and remain under their own license.

The moral right of the author has been asserted

Set in Avenir Light and Trajan Pro

Designed by Peter Fritz Walter

ISBN 978-1-984070-33-3

Publishing Categories
Law / Child Advocacy

Publisher Contact Information
publisher@sirius-c-publishing.com
http://sirius-c-publishing.com

Author Contact Information
pfw@peterfritzwalter.com

About Dr. Peter Fritz Walter
http://peterfritzwalter.com

About the Author

Parallel to an international law career in Germany, Switzerland and the United States, Dr. Peter Fritz Walter (Pierre) focused upon fine art, cookery, astrology, musical performance, social sciences and humanities.

He started writing essays as an adolescent and received a high school award for creative writing and editorial work for the school magazine.

After finalizing his law diplomas, he graduated with an LL.M. in European Integration at Saarland University, Germany, in 1982, and with a Doctor of Law title from University of Geneva, Switzerland, in 1987.

He then took courses in psychology at the University of Geneva and interviewed a number of psychotherapists in Lausanne and Geneva, Switzerland. His interest was intensified through a hypnotherapy with an Ericksonian American hypnotherapist in Lausanne. This led him to the recovery and healing of his inner child.

After a second career as a corporate trainer and personal coach, Pierre retired in 2004 as a full-time writer, philosopher and consultant.

His nonfiction books emphasize a systemic, holistic, cross-cultural and interdisciplinary perspective, while his fiction works and short stories focus upon education, philosophy, perennial wisdom, and the poetic formulation of an integrative worldview.

Pierre is a German-French bilingual native speaker and writes English as his 4th language after German, Latin and French. He also reads source literature for his research works in Spanish, Italian, Portuguese, and Dutch. In addition, Pierre has notions of Thai, Khmer, Chinese, Japanese, and Vietnamese.

All of Pierre's books are hand-crafted and self-published, designed by the author. Pierre publishes via his Delaware company, Sirius-C Media Galaxy LLC, and under the imprints of IPUBLICA and SCM (Sirius-C Media).

The author's profits from this book are being donated to charity.

Contents

Introduction — 9
Constitutional Considerations

Chapter One — 25
The Legal Split

Chapter Two — 67
Overcoming the Split

Chapter Three — 93
Child Protection Draft Bill
- §1 Preliminaries — 93
- §2 Competencies of Consultants — 95
- §3 Measures taken by Consultants — 96
- §4 Definitions — 100
- §5 Violence against Children — 103
- §6 Consent — 107
- §7 Degree of Violence & Burden of Proof — 113
- §8 Family & Educational Relations — 113

Bibliography — 119
Contextual Bibliography

Personal Notes — 139

Introduction

Constitutional Considerations

This study on sex laws, written by a lawyer, may appear uncanny. A closer regard on the history and content of sex laws shall reveal why not only trial lawyers today should be concerned about the legitimacy of such statutory trash.

In fact, also psychologists, psychiatrists, teachers, day care workers and, last not least, politicians, should share my concern.

If, for example, a statute defines as rape *any act of penetrating the female sexual organ by the male sexual organ*, the deep penetration of a woman's sexual organ with a vibrator could not, and in no way, be 'interpreted' as rape. Here civil law and criminal law largely differ because under civil law the use of the vibrator could be *interpreted* in such a way that it grossly boils down to what the legislator had in mind.

THE LEGAL SPLIT IN CHILD PROTECTION

Under criminal law however, a judge cannot voluntarily expand the scope of a provision without violating the constitutional principle of *nulla poena sine lege (due process)*. Male sexual organ is male sexual organ. And not vibrator. Period. If the judge *subsumed* the vibrator nonetheless under the *term* of rape, the criminal judgment, if it had taken place in Germany, could be attacked at the *German Constitutional Court,* and as a result would be nullified.

In the United States, the judgment could be attacked at the *United States Supreme Court. Nulla poena* is an important constitutional principle which says that nobody can be subjected to a criminal trial without the prior existence of a written law in precise wording under which the behavior in question can be subsumed.

This is why this principle is really *constitutional* and not just a law among laws. It's a superior principle in a constitutional democracy because in totalitarian regimes typically people are condemned by laws that either do not exist or that are applied against their precise wording, or by *extending their wording*, with the purpose namely to have people disappear from

INTRODUCTION

the political agenda. If a democracy is not only on paper, there typically is a *Constitutional Court* to supervise the whole legal system for constitutional guarantees to be applied and safeguarded by all involved in the law profession, including the law maker.

The *German Constitutional Court* has repeatedly invalidated criminal law bills that had passed parliament and that were thus valid laws. But because these laws were too general in their wording and not precise enough, they violated the principle *nulla poena sine lege*. As a result, the laws have been invalidated by the court and the prisoners condemned under these laws liberated and financially compensated for the injustice done to them.

So far for the constitutional principle. As we shall see in this study, this principle is so much violated, at least in Anglo-Saxon criminal jurisdiction, that we can speak of a reversal of rule and exception. While the rule is that penal laws must be precise to be constitutional, the legal reality in matters of sex laws is rather the contrary.

Sex laws are pitifully vague and therefore bear an increasing chance to be found unconstitutional and

THE LEGAL SPLIT IN CHILD PROTECTION

thus invalid, if only people would fight a case through until the Supreme Court.

Before the shift from liberalism to fascism after 1996 in most Western countries, the reform of age-of-consent laws was a serious issue of discussion in various national parliaments, such as for example the Italian, the German and the Dutch parliaments.

In Germany, the *Green Party* came up with the proposal to lower the age of consent to fourteen years of age. In Holland, already before that time, while the legal age of consent was sixteen, police did not persecute *sua sponte* any contravention, when the child was more than *twelve years* old. Only in case that both parents and child submitted a written demand for criminal persecution, the police enforced the law—in all other cases *not*.

Another point of discussion were same-sex contacts between adults and children. It was here precisely about the question if same-sex pedosexual contacts should eventually be treated in the same way as other pedosexual contacts. Traditionally, even in Holland, they were treated differently. And in most states of the United States, they are treated differently as well. For example in Georgia, the age of consent for girls is eighteen, for boys twenty-one.

As there is no rational basis for this discrimination of same-sex pedoerotic contacts, most parliament committees wanted to abolish them, as they had been abolished in Holland after the spectacular intervention of Senator Dr. Edward Brongersma who was charged with a six-months prison sentence for having had sex with a boy of sixteen years of age.

However, Brongersma fought against the judgment and eventually won the legal action against the Dutch Government; as a result criminal law was changed to abolish any difference between heterosexual and homosexual relations between adults and minors. It is obvious that the mere *lowering of ages of consent* has little or nothing to do with paradigm change. This kind of liberalization rests with the old repressive patriarchal paradigm.

Let us have a look what ages of consent are good for, or *supposed* to be good for! What is the idea behind segregating age groups and why is sexuality not allowed among all age groups? Why do laws almost everywhere rigidly fix certain ages for sex, and do not by contrast ask if sexual activity was constructive or damaging, peaceful or violent, coercive or consenting?

Law experts tend to argue that strict age of consent laws were assuring *legal clarity* as it was not to make out for every individual what were the conditions of a positive or negative sexual relation for a child, and that only psychologists could know the truth in this respect. And that, therefore, the law retreated, not daring to venture into psychological areas that it could not handle after all. I had several of my lawyer colleagues advancing this argument that upon further inquiry revealed to be barely correct. The true answer is that age of consent laws have merely *historical reasons*: they were the successors of Canonical statutes, of Church law that preceded state law in all Western cultures.

The legal history of sex laws very vividly illustrates why sex laws, from a lawyer's perspective, must be judged as problematic from a constitutional point of view.

Sex laws came up, for the first time in history, under the highly violent and arbitrary regime of *King Hammurabi (1792-1750 B.C.)*, sixth king of the *Amorite Dynasty* of Old Babylon.

INTRODUCTION

Sex laws then continued their existence under the violent doctrinaire regime of the Church that, organizing the first holocaust, persecuted, tortured and murdered hundreds of thousands of people in Europe and the early European colonies overseas, which represented a substantial slice of the populations.

Sex laws found their way to us not because they are felt to be *right and just*, but because of the mere fact that a law that is in place will not by itself get out of place.

You may know that laws can be unjust, arbitrary, discriminating and totally counterproductive in many ways, whilst this knowledge is usually not taught in school. But we know this from history. I could cite many examples. Laws, for instance, that say blacks enjoy a lesser standard of civil rights than white people, are discriminating laws. And from there I extrapolate the general principle that laws are not just potatoes that bother nobody and quietly sit in the ground until they are eaten. No, the reality is that laws *do bother people*. States do bother citizens. And I say *sex laws* are not potatoes because they are not just laws, but a perversity. They are a form of legislative perversion. *Sex laws* have no place in any form of real democracy, be it state-owned or people-owned. This is so because sex laws are making a crime of what are natural forms of human conduct. Sex laws, then, are not a matter of rational law policy, but an outflow of immaturity, of fear and of a refusal to take responsibility.

In last resort, and that is why conscious lawyers are hardly ever tranquil here, sex laws, because of their lack of precise wording of what actually constitutes the *crime* and what is the *victim* of the crime, are very problematic from a point of view of constitutional guarantees.

What has the state, the collective power, to do with love, *human love*, whatever this love be like? I really think and feel that most people are just too dull to be able to ask these and other pertinent questions. Because they just take all and everything for granted and, first of all, do not question *established power*.

Yet there is and will never be human freedom when power is not questioned, and *constantly* questioned.

For there is only a tiny step from power to tyranny.

INTRODUCTION

Only a critical mind, or a number of critical minds, by their very vigilance regarding power abuses, can prevent totalitarian forms of leadership and abusive state power to spread and become dominant.

The whole bulk of sex laws *has no right of existence* in a modern state that is based on democratic rights and a basic amount of privacy and personal freedom. Their coming into existence, as I have shown in my essay *Minotaur Unveiled*, was the result of the terror of the Church and all human rights abuses, murders and holocausts it committed over several hundred years in the whole of Europe. Without that sad chapter in the development of human consciousness, sex laws would probably never have come to existence in the first place.

> —See Peter Fritz Walter, Minotaur Unveiled: The Truncated Account of Adult-Child Erotic Attraction (Essays on Law, Policy and Psychiatry, Vol. 5, 2018).

And there is another observation that law experts usually engage in when evaluating a statute: it's *legal policy*. What is legal policy?

Legal policy, in simple terms, is *how laws affect people and their lives*, how laws achieve the goals and objectives they are made for, and how, or not, laws are respected by citizens. It may appear obvious that legal policy is very important, and perhaps more important to consider for the law maker than the actual drafting of the statutes. Thus, from a law policy point of view, experts agree that nobody is inclined to follow legal rules and statutes that are off-track, irrational, ineffective, unjust or arbitrary.

This principle is equally valid for alcohol or drug prohibitions. There appears to be a paradox: prohibitions contain an invisible time-bomb, something like a hypnotic command to be violated. Even when there is exorbitant or draconic punishment waiting for the law breaker, this basic state of affairs does not change. This is logically so because it has nothing to do with law, but with psychology. And laws that rule outside of the laws of psychology are simply silly. They are broken before they are in force.

Democracy can be measured upon the scale of its prohibitory statutes. A system that regards its members as irresponsible vassals will tend to rule *all and everything about them*, conceding to them but a *residual amount of personal freedom*. Such a system will try to impose strict inflexible rules of conduct upon each individual and leave it to the justice system to deal with those who offend the official order. Anglo-Saxon legal terminology is in this respect revealing in that it speaks of the *offender* and the *sex offender*.

These terms show evidently that criminal law actually retaliates against people who *offend* the system and that it is a mere pretense that criminal law *protected* the individual victim. Thus, we are still with one leg in the Middle-Ages. Besides that, the term *sex offender* is outright ridiculous: nobody can offend sex, and sex cannot offend the system. So *who does offend what* in this truly criminal terminology? By contrast, a society that basically trusts its individuals will formulate its criminal laws only as a regulatory means and *ultima ratio* for cases of extreme, violent or highly dangerous behavior.

Since violence is violence regardless of the form it takes, a democratic society will treat sexual violence as violence, and *not* as illicit sex.

And it will abstain from ruling into love and sexuality as basic forms of human expression and togetherness. It will thus restrict its intervention into intimacy to cases where violence is superimposed upon sex or linked to sex in a way that sex becomes a *weapon to overpower, subdue or humiliate another.* Thus, the target behavior for criminal laws, in a true democracy, will be violence, and not sex.

This is so because it's violence that does harm, not sex. And it's only harm that is the focal point of a state's intervention into the lives of citizens, and that grants the government the ultimate justification for such interference. When no harm is done, such interference would be arbitrary or unnecessary, or this power could be used in undemocratic ways.

That is why under the draft bill annexed to this study, only violence or harm done to children is the focal point of intervention, not any dubious concept of *public morality*, as it today still is applied in our sex laws and which meets with more and more open resistance from the side of trial lawyers.

From the moment we liberalize sexuality from its moralistic stigma that is a residue of inquisitory Church laws and therefore an anachronism in a modern legal system, we have no choice but to admit that human sexuality cannot reasonably be a subject to governmental regulation and interference. As a result, we must conclude that age-of-consent laws do not fit in a democratic society because they are not rationally verifiable and therefore represent a tool for paternalistic control and enslavement of the child's private life and desires. And in addition, they are completely ineffective to prevent the most chaotic and psychotic forms of sexual violence against children, including kidnapping and murder, which is a fact known from the daily news.

A new and democratic legal bill, if ever the criminal law system remains in place, must target upon *violence* and not sex, and incriminate both physical and sexual violence, not more and not less. Since in both physical and sexual assault, violence is the determining factor of the offense, it is more effective to treat *both kinds of offenses in one and the same legal bill* and not, as it is now, in a range of largely diverse bodies of laws that are distinct from each other and present no congruent scheme and hardly any synergies.

As the word *violence* has a rather ambiguous meaning, the present bill uses the term *harm* to precisely define what is the rationale of this bill. Harm is a term *which is well-defined* and it can be verified in each case, using empirical methods of scrutiny, if or not there was harm done to a child.

THE LEGAL SPLIT IN CHILD PROTECTION

The second point where this new legal bill should differ from previous legislation is that harm done against adults, be it physical or sexual harm, on one hand, and against children, on the other, should be treated in one and the same bill, and not in different and divergent laws.

The reasons for incriminating violence are exactly the same whether the violent assault is directed against an adult or against a child. Violence is violence, no matter against which members of the community it is released or inflicted. On the other hand, there is no rationale to incriminate *consenting love and sex* between generations whatever the age of the partners may be. What we need is a unified legal situation that leaves sex up to private enjoyment and focuses upon violence and actual harm done, and that treats both physical and sexual violence in one and the same bill.

So far, many legal experts agree.

But few of them will follow me when I do the next move that in my opinion is logical and that sets out to decriminalize the whole area of human behavior when matters of intimacy and sexuality are concerned. And this independently of the age of the persons involved in such intimacy and sexuality.

As a consequence of thinking the matter through until the end, we should take intimacy out of the hands of all state authorities and give control, if ever it is justified, over to legally empowered and incorporated consulting agencies.

Chapter One

The Legal Split

I can only throw a tiny spot on the immense jurisprudence dealing with the delicate topic of *legal corporal punishment* versus *illegal child battery*.

For the purposes of this study, it will suffice to summarize the basic findings on both and get at an integrative conclusion. Of course, the limitation of this study on the Anglo-Saxon legal system bears no preclusion, nor prejudice or value judgment with regard to an international perspective.

The Anglo-Saxon criminal law system is indeed the least representative because it is based on a Puritan, sex-denying and pleasure-hostile, and strongly violence-inducing value system.

If this research was going to be undertaken from a truly international perspective, a quite extensive and

THE LEGAL SPLIT IN CHILD PROTECTION

complex comparative law study would require a minimum of several years and considerable resources.

But the effort would be worth it and the results, probably, highly interesting. I suppose it would confirm my observation that the Anglo-American criminal law and correction system is *one of the most repressive* in the world, and one of the most cruel and inhuman that man ever has put on stage – next to the Church's Inquisition and Nazi concentration camps.

> —Adolf Hitler (1889-1945) was the Chancellor of Germany from 1933, and the Führer (Leader) of Germany from 1934 until his death. He was leader of the National Socialist German Workers Party (Nationalsozialistische Deutsche Arbeiterpartei or NSDAP), better known as the Nazi Party. Hitler gained power in a Germany facing crisis after World War I. Using propaganda and charismatic oratory, he was able to appeal to the economic need of the lower and middle classes, while sounding resonant chords of nationalism, anti-Semitism and anti-communism. With the establishment of a restructured economy, a rearmed military, and a totalitarian regime, Hitler pursued an aggressive foreign policy with the intention of expanding German Lebensraum (living space), which triggered World War II when Germany invaded Poland. At its greatest extent, Nazi Germany occupied most of Europe, but along with the other Axis Powers it was eventually defeated by the Allies. By then, Hitler's racial policies had culminated in the mass-murder of approximately eleven million people, including the planned genocide of about six million Jews, in what is now known as the Holocaust.

THE LEGAL SPLIT

It is a matter of common knowledge that so-called *physical* or *corporal* punishment as well as sex laws regarding children vary from culture to culture.

Cross-cultural studies on the practice of corporal punishment such as James W. Prescott's paper *Body Pleasure and the Origins of Violence (1975)* have come to the result that it is the combination of patriarchal values, a monotheistic religion with one single male god, the early deprivation of tactile nutrition and the prohibition of premarital sex that leads to violence, and thus also to violence against children, especially in its socially sanctified form as corporal punishment which is structural violence at its best.

In fact, we are here facing customs, traditions and social mores that have become legalized, thus making the strangest body of *law* in human history.

Of course, because of the limited scope of my research, the legal rules presented and discussed here can only serve as examples. In the United States, like in many other countries, the corporal punishment of children is generally accepted and more or less widely practiced.

THE LEGAL SPLIT IN CHILD PROTECTION

—Dean M. Herman, A Statutory Proposal to Prohibit the Infliction of Violence upon Children, 19 FAMILY LAW QUARTERLY, 1986, 1-52.

As a result, criminal justice assumes the task to define the limits where lawful corporal punishment exceeds into the huge grey zone of unlawful child battery. As the judge considers the social rules in this field as a kind of guideline, and since these social rules change constant over time, it is inevitable that the law in this matter is constantly shifting as well.

Besides this *time factor*, there is also a *territorial factor*. A judge in a small town in Texas may rule in a different way than a judge in, say, Boston or New York, simply because *social mores* differ with regard to the limits of physical punishment and the values attributed to paternal correction.

Please note that this is not a fault of the laws nor can it be held that the Texas judge is less qualified to rule about the matter. The fact simply is that the law in this field is not exact, but that criminal justice has that characteristics about it that it is always also to a large extent a matter of social and cultural considerations. Thus, criminal law, in this area, gives a considerable discretion to the judge, the jury and the prosecution *to incriminate certain behavior*, or *not incriminate* it.

It is for this reason that a total abolishment of corporal punishment of children has been suggested.

The general formula under the present state of the law is that corporal punishment of children by their parents or persons *in loco parentis* is not unlawful if it is *administered in good faith with parental affection, ... and not cruel or merciless.*

If this sounds reassuring, one might doubt when reading *Wharton's Criminal Law* textbook:

> According to some courts, the punishment is unlawful only if permanent injury results; a parent is not liable for excessive or even cruel punishment if he acted in good faith.
>
> —Wharton's Criminal Law, 14th ed. by Charles E. Torcia, Vol. II, §§99-282, Rochester, New York: The Lawyers Cooperative Publishing Co., 1979, p. 310.

This law is criminal indeed since it says: *Thou shalt not beat them to lifelong cripples; but as long as the damage you do to them or the torture you inflict upon them can be repaired, you can impudently massacre them.*

THE LEGAL SPLIT IN CHILD PROTECTION

And what does the chewing-gum clause *'in good faith'* do here? In the precedent *People v. Green (1909)*, the offender was charged with assault and battery of his adopted child *Mabel*, a twelve-year old girl. In the following case report, the offender is called *respondent*, and the girl *complaining witness*:

> On the day in question, …, respondent missed a 50-cent piece, and charged the complaining witness with its theft. She, however, denied having taken the money, whereupon the girl was disrobed, partially by Mrs. Green and partially by herself, and when she was naked and alone with the respondent was whipped by the respondent with a small riding whip. The respondent then tied her hands behind her back, having placed her nightgown on her, and left her. She was kept so tied from Friday afternoon until Sunday about noon, during which time the respondent fed her upon bread and water. On the Sunday morning following the whipping, the respondent and his wife left Mabel alone and went into the country. During Sunday forenoon she made some outcry and attracted the attention of Mrs. Jennie Wilton, who lived in the house adjoining respondent's. Mrs. Wilton notified some firemen in the engine house nearby, and the girl was taken naked and with her hands still tied from the room through the upstairs window of respondent's residence into the home of Mrs. Wilton. From there she was taken to the police headquarters and placed in the charge of Mrs. Francis Stoddard, the matron. Her condition is described by the matron as

follows: 'From here to the bend of the knee (illustrating) was so thick with marks, and underneath the marks the flesh was dark blue, green, curdled, and over that was the lashes, every one as large as my little finger, that was raised on her body. Across the abdomen, the lower limbs, was six marks, cut, where the blood oozed out and scabbed over. Seventy marks across here (indicating) that was not cut, but these six were cut. Had broken the skin and also across the lower limbs here, until the blood had oozed out, and scabbed over, and when I bathed the little thing with witch-hazel and water she cried, and I could not bathe them any more.' (119 NW 1087, 1087-1088)

It should be noted that in this case the *Supreme Court of Michigan* ruled that the limits of lawful corporal punishment were indeed exceeded, and that the respondent was liable of *child battery*. But it is noteworthy to see for what *reasons* the court came to this conclusion.

Contrary to what one may think, it was not the fact that the girl had been maltreated in a severe way by her foster father, *but the fact only that she had been naked* during the assault. It was not the lashes big as a little finger, it was not the pain inflicted on her, it was not the fact that her skin was broke and the blood oozed out at various spots, it was not the cruel imprisoning of the child during a whole weekend, it was not the fact that she had been tied up and put on a hunger diet.

It was the fact that she had been stripped before she was violently assaulted:

> We think one of the most serious elements of the respondent's offense is the conceded fact that he compelled the complaining witness, a female between 12 and 13 years of age, to stand before him nude and receive the castigation. This act is tended to shock her modesty, to break down her sense of decency and the inviolability of her person, which is the most valuable possession of a young girl. (Id., p. 1090).

This clearly means that if she had been assaulted *with her nightgown on*, all would have been okay. No word about the serious wounds and all the horrible suffering the girl was subjected to.

It was the extravagant component of her *nakedness*, a subtly sexual connotation, that was decisive for the judges to hold that she was mistreated.

It was *not* the excessive degree of violence, not the sadistic brutality and merciless treatment she was subjected to by her adoptive father.

How could the authoritarian paternalistic attitude of the judges be better expressed than in the words they used: *modesty, sense of decency?*

It is obvious that for these judges, the slightest sexual tenderness between the girl and her adoptive father would have been held ten times as harmful as the brutal assault and the impudent violation of her corporal integrity.

This is even more apparent, although in some hidden way, in the final statement of the court:

> It is not the intention of the court to in any way weaken parental authority. On the contrary, we hold that it is the unquestionable right of parents and those *in loco parentis* to administer such reasonable and timely punishment as may be necessary to correct growing fruits in young children; but this right can never be used as a cloak for the exercise of malevolence or the exhibition of unbridled passion on the part of a parent. (Id.)

In another precedent, *State v. McDonie (1924)*, the *West Virginia Supreme Court of Appeals* had to deal with an action against the mother of a six-year old boy who was cruelly mistreated by his step-father. The mother not only tolerated the brutal assault on the little boy, but it was proved that—

THE LEGAL SPLIT IN CHILD PROTECTION

> ... she fully and freely acquiesced in the cruel punishment inflicted on her son by the stepfather; that she brought the rods and switches used and stood by, not only without any attempt of interfere, but apparently aiding her husband in every way, as testified to by a witness present at the time. (37 ALR 699, 700)

Here is the case report:

> It appears that on the evening before the particular occurrence which led to the arrest of the defendant and her husband, the boy had absented himself from home, and was found at the home of his grand-father, the father of Mrs. McDonie, and brought home sometime just after midnight by an uncle. Mrs. Cassler says that after the uncle had gone, Joe McDonie brought in a bundle of switches and handed them to the boy, who in turn gave them to her. She says there were ten of them, and the smallest was as large as her largest finger. That then McDonie began whipping the boy in the dining room, and slung him against the wall, while defendant sat there and witnessed the assault; that the child ran upstairs, followed by McDonie, and that she and defendant followed them up; that the husband ordered the boy to get into the bathtub and take his clothing off, which he did, and then turned the hot water on; that all the time the child was pleading with the mother to take him out, and tried to turn the water off himself, but the husband threw him back several times brutally against the side of the tub; that *they* tied the child's hands behind him, and McDonie whipped him while he was in the hot water and held his head under the

THE LEGAL SPLIT

water until he strangled and bubbles arose to the surface; that defendant appeared to be no more concerned than if *it was whipping a dog, and she would smile at me*; that the child continually appealed to his mother to take him out; and that the only time Mrs. McDonie was not present was when she went after more sticks. Witness says that she afterward talked to defendant about McDonie's treatment of the child, and that defendant said she loved Joe better than she did the child. This witness had been living in the house with the McDonies about two weeks and says that during that time Joe McDonie whipped the child brutally almost daily; and that several times defendant asked him to whip it. (Id., p. 701).

There is hardly anything to comment on this *concerted action* of brutality from the part of the three adults, including the passive cold-blooded witness, against that poor little child. The witness speaks of the child as an *it*, not a *him* or *her*, as if speaking about a thing and not about a person. The Calvinistic worldview of conceiving children as strange and somewhat *devilish objects* when disobeying becomes clear in this case.

There is a pretty list of precedents cited in the case report after the following statement:

Inasmuch as defendant was the parent of James M. Gibson, she had a right to punish him, so that even if

> malice is presumed, in order to justify the conviction, the statute requires that the acts must have been done not only maliciously and unlawfully, but with the intent existing at the time the punishment was inflicted, either to maim, disfigure, disable, or kill. (Id., p. 700)

These conditions evidently show that a parent's discretion for crippling and disfiguring a child for lifetime is virtually unlimited. For how can *the intention to maim, disfigure, disable or kill* ever been proved at evidence for a court since it is a purely inner intention?

Another case, *State of Wyoming v. Spiegel (1928) (39 Wyo 309, 270 P 1064, 64 ALR 289)* states the following point of departure:

> For a parent or one standing in such place to strike a child in punishment for disobedience or other misconduct is not an assault and battery, but is the exercise of a legal right.

One may think that, over time, the judicial and social standards for admitting battery have changed. However, the Anglo-American legal system with its principle of *stare decisis*, the rigid adherence to often age-old judicial precedents does not favor flexible adaptation of legal rules to factual changes in the value system.

THE LEGAL SPLIT

Only statutory legislation that expressly overrides judicial precedents can bring effective change! In addition we have to doubt if social standards regarding parental and educational violence against children have really changed in any significant way since the 1920's.

The fact that these precedents with the cited commentaries are to be found in a 1979 treatise on criminal law does not encourage a positive answer to this question. *Wharton's Criminal Law* expressly states:

> A parent has the right to administer proper and reasonable chastisement to his child without being guilty of a battery. (Id., p. 309)

In good English, this means a parent has the legal right to inflict violence on a child, as far as this violence is *proper and reasonable*. Proper violence, proper wars and proper bombs.

Reasonable violence, reasonable casualties, reasonable weapons. The structural violence in this vocabulary speaks for itself.

With regard to the U.K., Cross and Jones' *Introduction to Criminal Law* states that the use of force does not constitute an assault or a battery if *the accused is acting in the exercise of the right of corporal punishment.*

> —Sir Rupert Cross, Introduction to Criminal Law, 10th Edition, London: Butterworth's, 1984, p. 134.

The definition is similar to the one used by American courts and the precedents cited under this judgment date from 1860, 1869, 1873 and 1934. One is from 1973. Obviously, a hundred years did not alter very much in a value system that considers the child the devil in person.

After all, educational violence against children appears to be a rather stable institution in so-called civilized nations. With regard to the *corporal chastisement* of pupils by their school teachers, the general formula under the common law was:

> At common law, a schoolmaster or teacher possessed discretionary power to inflict punishment upon his pupils and was not liable for battery in so doing unless the punishment caused permanent injury, was inflicted arbitrarily and without proper cause or maliciously. (Wharton, op.cit., p. 311)

The more recent opinion of the *United States Supreme Court* in the case *Ingraham v. Wright (430 US 651, 97 S.Ct. 1401, 51 L.Ed.2d 711)* may reflect the present state of the law:

THE LEGAL SPLIT

> The use of corporal punishment in this country as a means of disciplining schoolchildren dates back to the colonial period. It has survived the transformation of primary and secondary education from the colonials' reliance on optional private arrangements to our present system of compulsory education and dependence on public schools. Despite the general abandonment of corporal punishment as a means of punishing criminal offenders, the practice continues to play a role in the public education of schoolchildren in most parts of the country. Professional and public opinion is sharply divided on the practice, and has been for more than a century. Yet we can discern no trend toward its elimination. At common law a single principle has governed the use of corporal punishment since before the American Revolution; teachers may impose reasonable but not excessive force to discipline a child. (…) Although the early cases viewed the authority of the teacher as deriving from the parents, the concept of parental delegation has been replaced by the view – more consonant with compulsory education laws – that the State itself may impose such corporal punishment as is reasonably necessary *for the proper education of the child and for the maintenance of group discipline.* (Id.)

What was abandoned as a humiliating practice against criminal offenders *is still good enough for treating school children!* If we only replace the word *force* in the text of the judgment with the word *violence*, one of its sentences reads as follows:

THE LEGAL SPLIT IN CHILD PROTECTION

'[T]eachers may impose reasonable but not excessive violence to discipline a child...'.

Group discipline appears for the Supreme Court to have such a high importance that it justifies group violence. Violence as a social sanction is thus, according to the Supreme Court, a proper means to regulate social relations. And a trend *for elimination* of group violence, and all violence, will, according to this judgment, evidently not come from the jurisprudence.

The following survey over present sexual laws involving children will show that these laws treat both violent and non-violent sex with children in exactly the same way. The rationale behind these laws evidently is the *sinful character of sex*, not the destructive consequences of violence inflicted upon a child.

This is not surprising after all since present sexual laws have their roots in century-old *Canon Law*, a legal body created by the Christian Church and which was founded on moralistic rather than humanitarian principles. After all, it was not the integrity of children that those laws were supposed to protect, but the child as a part of her father's possession. Thus, *the child as a person had no legal status*; his or her legal

THE LEGAL SPLIT

status was a mere derivation from the legal status of their father. It is very important to keep this in mind when reviewing present sexual laws for they are drafted from this fundamental perspective, and not from our perspective as 21st century citizens with our focus on the child's ultimate welfare.

This is especially important when we deal with terms such as *purity* or *innocence, decency* or *moral integrity* for these terms actually let see that the object of protection is not the child or the child's physical integrity, but a *societal, cultural, ideal or religious value called morality*—whatever this is. While the sexual purity or innocence of a child is historically a relatively recent idea.

> —Unlawful Sex: Offences, Victims and Offenders in the Criminal Justice System of England and Wales, The Report of the Howard League Working Party, London: Waterloo Publishers Ltd., 1985, p. 20.

This idea may have some importance within the Christian value system, but today, and here is the distortion, the mass media suggest that the mythical notion of children's purity was a *fact*, while renowned progressive child psychologists such as *Alayne Yates* affirm that the child's sexual purity is a *pure myth*.

THE LEGAL SPLIT IN CHILD PROTECTION

—Alayne Yates, Sex Without Shame, New York, 1978.

Yet our outdated sexual laws take it for granted that a child has to be 'protected' from fully experiencing the most pleasurable side of life. If we look for possible reasons why sex and violence have become linked historically, there may be one that most researchers, until now, have overlooked.

Many a brutal attack against a child is perpetrated by parents or educators exactly because children revolt against the innocence terror imposed on them by our life-denying culture, and search to engage in what is forbidden: they tend to actively pursue to have sex with peers or adults they love.

And how ferocious punishments habitually are for this truly innocent reason, and how disproportionate they regularly are is a matter of common knowledge. *Alexander Sutherland Neill*, the founder of the famous *Summerhill School* in England reports in his autobiography a revealing incident of harsh punishment by his parents following sex play he had as a boy with his sister.

—Alexander Sutherland Neill, Neill! Neill! Orange-Peel!, New York: Hart Publishing Co., 1972.

THE LEGAL SPLIT

The traumatic effects of such early punishment for sex play and its lasting influence on the personality of the later adult have since long been discovered by psychoanalysis. To kill emotions means to kill life - and neurosis, depression, cancer and aids are some of the consequences.

Sex laws are among the most salient perversities in our legal body. Back in the dark ages, that were not so dark after all regarding child sexuality, children could consent to sex as early as at ten and usually married between twelve and fourteen years. And this despite the fact that puberty, because of poor nutrition, occurred much later than today, usually around fifteen. In the last two centuries, with a largely improved public health system, puberty occurred at about twelve years of age, and yet the consent of girls under sixteen was considered as legally invalid.

Today, in the Western world, puberty happens between ten and twelve years of age because of highly potent and hormone-rich nutrition, but a fifteen year old girl is forbidden to make love with her older boyfriend, lest the boy incurs to be charged with so-called *statutory rape*.

THE LEGAL SPLIT IN CHILD PROTECTION

Where is the logic of such legal policy? The fact is that there is no logic in sex laws because they are not made on the basis of rational reasoning but reflect purely irrational moralistic ideas that come from mostly non-legal sources such as folk wisdom, superstition and fear, at a time when serious scientists wondered how many angels could fit on the tip of a needle.

Three precedents by the *Supreme Court of Arkansas* in 1891, 1897 and 1904 show how *statutory rape* came to be recognized as a legal term. While, according to an early English statute, the original rule incorporated in American common law was *'if any person shall unlawfully and carnally know and abuse any woman-child under the age of ten years, it shall be a felony without clergy,'* later courts have extended more and more the term *'abuse of a woman-child'*. In the 1891 case, *Warner v. State (54 Ark 660, 17 SW 6)*, the *Supreme Court of Arkansas* still distinguished between rape as non-consenting intercourse which was punishable with death, and the *carnal and unlawful knowledge of a female child under the age of puberty* which was punishable between five and twenty-one years in the penitentiary.

THE LEGAL SPLIT

The court stated that *'[t]he crime of carnally knowing a female child under the age of puberty can be committed only where the victim is under twelve years old, and has sufficient intelligence to know the nature of the act, and to consent, and does consent thereto.'*

According to an earlier decision of the same court, puberty was deemed to begin with twelve years of age. In the case, the girl had been eleven-years old and the accused had submitted proof as to her consenting to intercourse.

—Coates v. State (1888), 7 SW 304.

In the 1897 case, *Bond v. State (63 Ark 504, 39 SW 554.)*, a new statute was considered which made punishable *carnal knowledge of a girl under sixteen years of age with or without her consent.*

Thus, the distinction between forcible rape defined as intercourse without consent, and consenting intercourse, which was still a basis of the 1891 precedent, was abandoned by the new statute. The result was that forcible rape, which is a form of sexual violence, became assimilated with consenting intercourse, a fact that is quite noteworthy as it is something that in any other body of law would outrage lawyers and judges! How can a statute be made that is deemed to bring even a slight form of legal progress, that puts violent child abuse in the form of forcible rape on one and the same foot with a fully consenting sexual relationship?

This is like treating apples and pears in the same way. Or, with other words: it proves the irresponsibility of the legislator. Because from the perspective of law policy, such a statute incites to commit violent sexual crimes! *Go out and rape!* this statute says. It's a legal absurdity. And yet nobody ever protested against these nonsensical and truly criminal laws, and that is what many lawyers find appalling.

This strange turn of the law had two consequences. The first one was that the former ultimate punishment in the form of the death penalty for forcible rape was lowered to the punishment of statutory rape. As a result, the rapist of an adult woman was punished much harder than the rapist of a girl under sixteen!

Secondly, consenting intercourse with girls aged twelve to sixteen became, for the first time in history, a crime!

THE LEGAL SPLIT

This is strange because the courts affirmed that puberty was happening at twelve whereas under the former liberal common law maturity happened much later. Thus the question remains open what in fact the new statute was to protect if not a pure morality principle?

In a 1904 case, *Plunkett v. State (72 Ark 409, 82 SW 845.)*, the *Supreme Court of Arkansas* used for the first time the new legal term *statutory rape* which is per definition no rape, but a *consenting sexual activity* that is legally deemed to be a rape-like offense. In the case the girl had been fifteen, and she had consented to intercourse and had born a baby. It was not certain that the accused was the father of the baby. But on a charge for statutory rape evidence that the girl had had sexual intercourse also with other men was not admissible. Thus, even if the girl had had regular sexual intercourse with other men and got the baby from another man, the accused would not have been able to construe a defense from this fact, a rather absurd result. This suggests that what the new law of statutory rape actually protected was a dubious notion of *public morals*, but not the *corporal integrity* of the child. The commentary notes:

THE LEGAL SPLIT IN CHILD PROTECTION

> Age 16 was chosen to cover that period of later adolescence when the chief significance of sexual behavior is its contravention of the moral standards of the community. (Ark Rev Stats Ann, § 510.060)

In good English: life and pleasure of children have to be sacrificed for perpetuating ideological values of a majority of sex-ignorant hypocrites. It is hard to find better evidence for the fact that sex laws serve the survival of institutionalized patriarchal societal structures and not the needs and wants of children!

This is further corroborated by the fact that the statute only punished *unlawful* sexual intercourse, and thus intercourse outside a valid marriage. At the time, girls could notably marry at age fourteen. Thus, had the accused married the girl before the intercourse happened, sex would have been lawful under the statute and no punishment had resulted from the intercourse. What, in fact, has all this to do with rape and sexual violence?

In addition, the laws in this area are of a vagueness that is probably unconstitutional. We have seen that rape and statutory rape were two distinct offenses and that statutory rape has nothing to do with *the forcible penetration of the female sexual organ against her will*, but that it typically is a *consenting*

THE LEGAL SPLIT

sexual activity between two persons of different age. It is therefore pure sophism and against the constitutional principle of *nulla poena sine lege* to classify consenting sexual relationships as rape-like offenses:

> Viewed conceptually, a female under a specified age is also deemed incapable of consenting and hence her apparent consent is treated as immaterial. (Ariz Rev Stats Ann, § 13-1401(3)

Not enough with this legal mess, certain States, as for example Arizona, also extended the term *sexual intercourse* to encompass *any manual masturbatory contact with the penis or vulva.*

—Wharton, op. cit., p. 65.

In good English: not only when the older boyfriend makes love with his fifteen-year old girlfriend, but already when he caresses manually her vaginal lips, and when they do this in Arizona, he has *raped her* in Arizona – statutorily, but nonetheless.

Viewed conceptually!

Such legal *conceptions* fit in the stone age and have no place in a civilized body of law based upon a precise wording and definition of what is punishable under the law.

The constitutional guarantee of *nulla poena sine lege* goes back to the *Magna Carta of 1215* that states in its §39:

> No freemen shall be taken or imprisoned or disseised or exiled or in any way destroyed, nor will we go upon him nor send upon him, except by the lawful judgment of his peers or by the law of the land.

This principle is further an integral part of the *United States Federal Constitution*. Yet it seems to have very little practical value within criminal justice in the United States if only the trial has a remote connection with sex. In Georgia, another statutory rape like offense is called *child molestation*:

> A person commits child molestation, with imprisonment from one to twenty years, when he does any immoral or indecent act to or in the presence of or with any child under the age of fourteen years with the intent to arouse or satisfy the sexual desires of either the child or the person.

Wharton notes that it is equally sufficient that the child touches the clothing covering the immediate area of the adult's intimate parts. (Id., p. 106) In good

THE LEGAL SPLIT

English: someone who in any way grants a child sexual pleasure, even if this person is the child's parent, in Georgia risks to be imprisoned for twenty years. For, *viewed conceptually*, to repeat it, the child has been 'raped' by having learnt how sexual excitement feels like.

This is only one example of many that demonstrate that it is not the child that is protected by sex laws, but the perpetuation of *adult sexual inhibitions* and a totally corrupt morality: it is considered a crime worth twenty years of prison to show a child having sexual pleasure!

In Georgia, it is a crime to *masturbate for hire*, which is to stimulate the sexual organs of a client by a masseur or masseuse. (Id.)

In California, *sexually assaulting an animal* is one vintage of *sodomy* and classified among *deviant sexual intercourse*. (Id., p. 92)

In Iowa, sexual contact with a child is a *lascivious act with a child*, in Illinois it is *indecent liberties with a child* or *contributing to the sexual delinquency of a child*. (Id., p. 113) This latter formulation is particularly significant. Not only that human sexuality destroys

THE LEGAL SPLIT IN CHILD PROTECTION

children and animals, it also renders children *delinquent*. The absurdity of these laws becomes particularly evident when compared to the jurisprudence on corporal punishment.

Such a comparison namely reveals how little this same society cares about the pain and the suffering inflicted upon a child 'in the name of their own best.' To tear up the skin of a small child with a whip, to blow the naked bottom of a child with a stick is lawful; to lick it tenderly is qualified as *anilingus* and is a criminal offense equated with *sexual penetration*, *deviate intercourse* or *sodomy* and punished with up to twenty years of prison.

—Wharton, op. cit., §297.

What to me only appears truly deviate here is the value system of a society that punishes pleasure and legally sanctions violence and brutality, while the statistics show the exactly opposite picture to be true. Statistics namely reveal a strong predominance of physical child abuse over sexual child abuse.

Such a legal system is structurally violent. The laws, the trials and the correction system are but a bad copy of the Church's *Inquisition* and have very

THE LEGAL SPLIT

little to do with a modern penal system. A society with such an aggression level has no mandate in protecting children against physical or sexual violence *for it is itself based upon violence.*

The *National Center on Child Abuse and Neglect* in Washington D.C. reported that in 1982, 311.500 US children were mistreated. Media coverage of this fact almost exclusively deals with sexual child abuse, yet the figures the Center provides clearly show the opposite perspective to be true: sexual abuse took place in only 7% of the 331.500 cases.

—Associated Press, March 31, 1984.

The history of sex laws involving children can very clearly be retraced in the Netherlands, after Sweden made the first step for abandoning corporal punishment. Sweden was among the first nations to abolish physical punishment in their public schools and in families. In fact, from 1979 *it is no longer allowed for anyone, including parents, to spank or otherwise physically punish children.*

The law has been welcomed by many Swedish child psychiatrists, psychologists, sociologists and doctors. In fact, the elaboration of new legal

THE LEGAL SPLIT IN CHILD PROTECTION

structures is not necessary in this area because there is only one justifiable solution: the total abandonment and prohibition of corporal punishment. The Sweden example shows that this only requires a responsible decision from the side of the legislator.

The new legal situation in Holland was outlined by Dr. Edward Brongersma, Dutch lawyer and Senator, in his 1981 course at *Berlin University* in Germany. The following information about the various Dutch sex law reforms were kindly provided for this book by Dr. Edward Brongersma, at that time *Senator of the Dutch House of Lords*, and thus himself involved in the reforms as a parliamentary member. The information was given to me in form of a type script entitled *Der Speijer-Report*, 1981, in German language, that Dr. Brongersma drafted for the course at *Berlin University. Until 1886 sex with children of both sexes was not punishable, in France until 1832.*

Homosexuality was punishable with the death penalty, but only in ecclesiastic courts. The same is true under common law with regard to *sodomy*.

—Wharton, op. cit., §§294 ff.

THE LEGAL SPLIT

It is typical for the Christian Church's act-centered mechanistic view of sexuality that sexual behavior was judged and classified according to the acts performed, and not as a physical form of human love.

As a result, under common law *sodomy* was defined as the *carnal copulation of persons in other than the natural manner.*

>—Wharton, op. cit., §295, 77.

Needless to mention that it was the Church who defined what was nature and what was not. Contrary to the Church's canon law, Montesquieu wrote in *L'Esprit des Lois* that society should only punish behavior that was harmful for its citizens, and not what was only against certain *moral feelings.*

>—Charles-Louis de Secondat, Baron de La Brède et de Montesquieu (1689-1755), more commonly known as Montesquieu, was a French social commentator and political thinker who lived during the Enlightenment. He is famous for his articulation of the theory of separation of powers, taken for granted in modern discussions of government and implemented in many constitutions throughout the world. He was largely responsible for the popularization of the terms feudalism and Byzantine Empire. L'Esprit des Lois (The Spirit of the Laws) is a book on political theory Montesquieu published in 1748. The book was influential, inter alia, on the drafting on the United States Constitution. Montesquieu suggested

that the governing body of a nation should be divided into three branches: the executive, the legislature, and the judiciary, possibly the first to ever suggest this. This concept is called the Separation of Powers.

From 1810 to 1886 the Netherlands' civil law statute was a translation of the French *Code Napoléon* under which non-violent intercourse was not punishable regardless of gender and age of the partners! Only after 1886, in the Netherlands' first own penal code, *Het Wetboek van Strafrecht*, an age of consent, fourteen years, was introduced.

It is interesting to know that, when the Dutch government made the legal draft for this bill, it was alleged that *terrible things had happened*, which means child abduction and the lustmurder of children.

Brongersma contradicted these allegations showing that in hindsight nothing could be found about this in the literature of the time. Thus, what we face here is some of the typical journalistic tactics that sabotage legal reform by the usual fascist smear propaganda. What was finally drafted was not legal reason, but political agendas, not responsible legal policy, but propaganda, and this led eventually Belgium and France (1832) equally changing their laws accordingly.

THE LEGAL SPLIT

While still in the Middle-Ages children of eleven years married and fourteen-year olds had leading jobs, this had become impossible with modern technology and industry and the resulting long educational cycles. To work was the highest ideal, and thus pleasure in the form of sex was made down as a murky, lazy, sordid, filthy, dirty and immoral activity. From this Puritan work ethics resulted the myth that children were *pure and innocent* because it exactly fit into the bourgeois ethics at the beginning of the *Industrial Revolution*.

I am not the only lawyer to contradict, in this respect, researchers who allege the turndown of child sexuality was an early result of patriarchy and thus occurred already five thousand years ago. These scientists overlook that patriarchy was not particularly focused upon child sexuality, and considered sexual feelings in children with worry only when they interfered with the father's *patria potestas*, thus typically when a girl reached puberty, because she then had to be married off as a matter of custom and also for mercantile reasons. Apart from the absolute taboo of girls' premarital virginity, there was no stigma upon child sexuality, children's sex play, or child-adult sexual activities.

Out of the proposed fourteen years as the age of consent became sixteen years in the parliamentary discussions. A minority in the *House of Commons* used the opportunity to propose punishment for homosexuality. But the majority refused with the argument that moralistic considerations had no place in a modern penal law.

This went on until 1968 when the *Speijer-Report* was drafted in which all myths about homosexuality were disproved with scientific references. In addition, it was stated that since it was known that children were not asexual, the opinion grew that the dangers resulting from sexual encounters involving children and adolescents had often been overestimated. In its conclusion, the expert commission stated that *seduction* did not play the role that most people attributed to it and that, even in cases where the adult initiated the child in the sexual activity, the child in many cases awaited from the adult to be initiated. This was found to be true for both homosexual and heterosexual encounters between children and adults. Finally it was stated that this initiation, in what sexual

THE LEGAL SPLIT

direction whatever it led, could in many cases contribute to a better development of the youth.

All this is explicated in an official document of the Dutch government. *Polak*, the Dutch Minister of Justice at this time, supported the report and made it a basis for a reform draft. The draft was so convincing that in the second chamber of the *Dutch House of Commons* only five members out of one hundred fifty voted against it. The *Dutch House of Lords* adopted the draft bill unanimously.

In October 1969, the Dutch parliament, according to the *Speijer-Report*, abolished the law that discriminated *homosexual pedophilia* thus fixing sixteen years as the appropriate age of consent for man-boy sexual relations, while formerly it was twenty-one.

In most countries, the discrimination of homosexual pedophilia is still existing, yet the ages of consent differ. In England, the *Indecency with Children Act 1960* makes punishable any act of indecency, or incitement to indecency, with or toward a child under fourteen, regardless of the sex of either the child or the offender. In addition, homosexual relationships are prohibited with persons under

THE LEGAL SPLIT IN CHILD PROTECTION

twenty-one years of age. The *Policy Advisory Committee on Sexual Offenses* (1981) has recommended that this age should be reduced to eighteen.

—Unlawful Sex, supra note 21, 8.26 and 8.29.

It is similar in Germany where the general age of consent is equated with the legal definition of child as *a person under fourteen years of age*, while there is a discrimination according to the nature of the relationship. While it's fourteen in general, it's sixteen in ascendancy relations, and eighteen in dependency relations, and equally eighteen for homosexual acts.

—Dreher & Tröndle, Strafgesetzbuch und Nebengesetze, 42. Aufl., München: Beck, 1985.

In France, non-violent pedophilia *(attentat à la pudeur sans violence)* with a child under fifteen years is punishable according to art. 331, al. 1er and 3 *Code Pénal* but also non-violent indecent acts on minors between fifteen and eighteen years if ascendancy relations are involved.

Equally homosexual acts with a minor between fifteen and eighteen years of age are punishable.

> —Roger Merle, Roger & André Vitu, Traité de Droit Criminel: Droit Pénal Spécial, Vol. II, par André Vitu, Paris: Editions Cujas, 1982.

In Denmark, the age of consent is fifteen for both sexes, without any further discrimination of homosexual acts. In Switzerland, the age of consent is sixteen, but there is much criticism in the literature and proposals are made to fix fourteen years as a more appropriate age limit.

> —Günter Stratenwerth, Schweizerisches Strafrecht: Besonderer Teil II, 3. Aufl., Bern: Stämpfli, 1984.

The same article, § 191, of the Swiss Penal Code treats both dependency and ascendancy relations as qualifications in punishment. Besides that, however, so-called homosexual seduction is even punishable with persons above sixteen years of age.

Now let us have a look at consensual relations. The reasons given in the European literature against even consensual sex with children are quite uniform: the child is supposedly to be *protected* of sexual pleasure in order not to become premature or disturbed in their psychosexual development.

The Dutch legislation, too, foresees a protection clause for homosexual relationships with minors over

THE LEGAL SPLIT IN CHILD PROTECTION

sixteen years of age. Such relations are still punishable when the prosecution can prove relevant danger to the child that was a consequence of the homosexual act and that would not have occurred in a heterosexual encounter. However, such cases are extremely rare. The scientific research upon which the *Speijer Report* was based revealed that by the 16th year the sexual propensity is developed to such an extent that a youngster who is heterosexual cannot be diverted by *seduction* into permanent homosexuality.

—Unlawful Sex, supra note 21, 4.17.

Before the fascist turndown in the Netherlands in 1996 as a result of conforming with American world puritanism, and resulting changes of the law, the prosecution and police forces did *not enforce the law* when the child was above twelve years old and when no claim was made by the child or their family to prosecute the adult lover. In about 66% of all cases known to the police, such a refusal of prosecution was practiced. However, it has to be seen that this information stems from the 1970's.

After the fundamentalist drift in the Netherlands in 1996, as a consequence of the worldwide *child abuse hysteria*, the situation changed to the exact contrary

THE LEGAL SPLIT

and the Netherlands have become one of the toughest countries in matters of so-called *child protection*.

Still in 1981, a petition of the Association of the work group for pedophilia and of the greatest Dutch association of primary school teachers was presented to the Dutch government aiming at the total abandonment of any age of consent in sexual laws. Another petition was presented in 1987 to the Dutch Minister of Justice proposing to specify conditions under which the prohibition did not apply, notably in those cases in which the child initiates or actively engages in the sexual activity. The petition was signed by a considerable number of persons including law professors, lawyers, prosecution attorneys, physicians, psychologists, psychiatrists, psychotherapists, sociologists, priests, authors, etc., and was a representative sample of the Dutch society. Moreover, the recommendations of the *Advisory Committee on Moral Legislation (Melai Committee)*, which were published in 1980, and the draft of a bill, presented to the Dutch cabinet in 1985 are worth to be mentioned.

The *Melai-Report* proposed that the prohibition of sex with persons under sixteen years of age, while excluding dependency relations, be changed into a prohibition of *sexual rapprochement* of such persons. The draft bill of 1985 contained a prohibition of sexual contacts with below sixteen-year olds that have been prepared or promoted by presenting or promising gifts, abuse of ascendancy or by deception. This decriminalization would only apply in non-dependency relations.

As in the Netherlands, the debate in France, Germany and Switzerland and other countries goes on for lowering the age of consent from sixteen to fourteen years of age.

Compared with pre-19th century laws however, a mere lowering of the age of consent seems to be a mere show case of a government's alleged *progressiveness* than a really effective solution.

Where is the justification for age fourteen? Why not thirteen, twelve or eleven? The question is if an age of consent has *any rationale* at all.

At least, when fixing the age of consent at the age of puberty, one could argue that puberty or sexual maturity was after all a *biological event* that can be considered as a justifiable landmark for reform drafts concerning the age of consent.

Chapter Two

Overcoming the Split

The research work on the topic of *violence against children* opened my eyes with regard to the *legal split in child protection* that today can be said to represent something like a unique example for judicial schizophrenia.

> —See Peter Fritz Walter, The Roots of Violence: Why Humans Are Not By Nature Violent (Essays on Law, Policy & Psychiatry, Vol. 12, 2018).

I became aware quite early that to resolve the legal split in child protection, we have to treat *both physical and sexual violence against children* in one and the same legal bill. This requires us to have a deeper look at what many still believe is necessary: *educational violence*. As long as a majority of citizens upholds the view that violence is good when it's educational, we probably can wait until the end of all times for a change in the law to happen here.

THE LEGAL SPLIT IN CHILD PROTECTION

The same people who tend to vote for upholding the physical punishment of children tend to affirm the righteousness of inflicting violence upon prisoners, and prisoners of war. They tend to justify *all* violence. Because they belittle violence, or are not aware of the long-term damages violence brings about for society as a whole. They have violence virtually in their bones. They have been nourished not with mother milk and love, but with father milk and *violence*, which is the only milk a father under patriarchy is supposed to give to his child, namely in the form of beatings, of whipping and of spanking.

In fact, the harmful effects of spanking have only recently been recognized internationally. It was not long ago that so-called *positive parenting* was recognized as something so important that it would receive government funding because it's a social policy *that works*.

According to a poll by iVillage in 2005, 73% found physical violence against children as a form of discipline either *'okay, when nothing else works'* or *'an effective type of discipline.'* This poll says more than well-sounding declarations. It says that the majority of Americans, while considering violence against adults as criminal, find violence against children okay when it serves to render children obedient. *This means that the concern for protecting the child against violence from the side of adults seems to be a hypocrite endeavor.*

This fact suggests that most American parents are not responsible citizens, but domestically violent. Furthermore, it indicates that American culture is not a peaceful culture, but rather something like a *primal horde* because it does *not* consider the child as a respected entity, but as a *slave* and *poison container*.

These people, and it's the majority in most of our modern industrial cultures, are not aware that violence brings decay, both in the individual life and in the life of a group, of a nation, of a country.

And the subject is even more complex: those same people who tend to uphold educational and state violence, *consider sex as something highly dangerous, something highly explosive, something that needs tight control and supervision.*

In much the same way they belittle violence, they make of sex a myth and instead of putting their minds into the true causes of violence, they worry about the

THE LEGAL SPLIT IN CHILD PROTECTION

silly daily right-or-wrong of sex. It's silly because sex is something natural. Violence not. But in their utter confusion, they are *unable* to see this truth. When we see that laws in a particular field are ineffective, arbitrary, irrational and silly and that they bring about more social confusion, more violence, more harmful behavior than at the time when those laws did not exist, why the hell do we want to uphold these laws?

My answer is simple. Because we are afraid of freedom. If there is something we are most afraid of, even abhor, it's freedom. Yet we pay lip service to the contrary. But that only confirms me right. We are prison-hungry, and like to be slave in a group of slaves. And we try to kill each and everybody who is feeling he's not a slave, but a king. Because, to repeat it, we, as a society, abhor true freedom. We argue that freedom brings chaos. That's so because we do not understand nature. Nature does not need *control* to be good. Nature brings about all living and maintains the sun to shine without needing governmental control or funding.

Nature has brought about sexual attraction. Man has brought about sexual violence. Nature has created pleasure, man does all to destroy it.

Nature has given us freedom, man does all to do away with it and establish unfreedom as the order of the day. Nature has instilled in children sexual curiosity, man has distilled age of consent laws – and without asking those who are concerned by these laws: the children.

Every age of consent is arbitrary in some way and dependent on the myth of children's innocence in sexual matters, as well as on ambiguous religious or cultural assumptions and customs.

Historical research brought to daylight that throughout human history, ages of consent constantly varied according to the economic and social context of a given society or community and the value system resulting from this context. It is since long disproved that it is the mere procreation ability that grants children competence and capacity for giving or receiving sexual pleasure.

Procreation capacity is not necessary for a child to being able to consent to body touch or for exchanging sensual pleasure with certain preferred persons whatever their age. Especially for children below the *age of reason*, the usual regard upon sex as a matter of *acts* and their distinction into

THE LEGAL SPLIT IN CHILD PROTECTION

non-penetrative and penetrative ones does not make sense. When a child is enamored with an adult, the child tends to express willingness also for a penetrative embrace, even if the child is physically not yet ready for intercourse. In the magic world of a small child, loving interaction with an adult is part of an *integrative* worldview that makes no difference between the nature of various pleasures, and where the *sexual game is a matter of fantasy*, not a factual understanding of its physical reality.

The actual willingness for full sexual intercourse often to be encountered with small girls who are enamored with an adult man is not surprising. It is not based upon what sexology calls the *facts of life*, but expression of that magical reality the small girl lives in and expresses in often poetic language. It does not bother about the size of the genitals that are going to be *put into each other*, while this may funnily be expressed that way, and it has no act-centered sexual opinions. It is based upon emotions, and the *flow* of emotions as a vital ingredient of love. It is beyond body poetics and rooted in the small child's encompassing magical reality. We may not yet fully understand child sexuality, but I think I can safely say that for the child the *magic anticipation* of intercourse is an *intrinsic element of psychosexual growth* and a sane expression of small children's fantasy world.

This psychological reality, to say this clearly, does *not* justify pedophilia as a political agenda, or a future political agenda. It asks for protecting the *magical space of the child* by not imposing educational control and supervision of the child's intimate sphere. It's, so to say, a principle of non-intervention that I advocate here. Or, to use the much simpler terms of Bob Marley: *Let the children play.*

Age of consent laws truly had some rationale in times where the actual age of puberty of a child coincided with a child's sexual and social maturity. This is historically thus valid for the Middle-Ages where it was with around *twelve to fourteen years* that a young person could consent to sexuality, marry and establish a business. In all later periods, and especially in modern times, an evident clash is to be noticed between the actual emosexual maturity of a child and his or her legal age of consent.

This brings about social and legal uncertainty and actually degrades children instead of helping them to mature functionally into responsible adults and interdependent members of the community.

Present age of consent laws inhibit children from natural sexual and non-sexual life experience and hold them imprisoned in an artificial *cocoon of immaturity* that retards and even disables the full expansive blooming of their bioenergetic and spiritual potential.

Research has shown that a rigid age of consent barrier as legal discrimination between unlawful sex or lawful sex with children is in practice of little functional value because of the differences in the actual development and maturity of every child. Instead, it has been seen that it is rather a matter of values why social groupings opt for more severe or else more liberal sex laws. It became particularly evident during the reform discussions in the Netherlands that it is not in children's best interest that reform is undertaken, but as a matter of political purpose and with the after-thought getting through with certain political goals.

Those who share liberal social views and emphasize the autonomy of the child tend to favor a low age of consent while those with traditional views and right-wing political orientation *tend to emphasize stricter sexual laws with a pronounced attitude to holding children back from autonomous decisions*, thus implicitly denying children's innate right for self-determination.

In principle children are able to give valid factual consent to sexual activities with adults, which includes being penetrated as part of a loving sexual embrace. This ability is independent of the child's age and not related to certain biological events such as puberty or sexual maturity, or else emission capacity. It is a mere question of *actual willingness*.

Besides that, it is a matter of culture and education if, or not, a child only shows sexual curiosity and engages in autoerotic sex play, or shares, more actively, in a fuller range of sexual interaction with others.

The assumption made by early psychoanalysis that sane children were *only* autoerotic and not able for partnership, is superseded by newer sexological research showing that children, when given freedom, will explore all that is sexually possible, including complete intercourse with *both* children *and* adults. It is *not* a matter of any fictive or legally recognized maturity.

Early psychoanalytic findings, such as those done by Sigmund Freud that seem to show that children tend to engage only in autoerotic sexual satisfaction were rendered under the spell of the highly puritan morality of the industrial bourgeoisie of that time. On the basis of the child's general capacity to give and receive pleasure, the child is able to decide in each instance what *feels right* and what *feels not right* regarding sex and love with oneself and others.

The fact that societal attitudes through the process of educational conditioning will influence the child's general attitude in sexual matters cannot be a reason to let societal interests devaluate the emotional and sexual needs of children.

Besides that, even the proponents of traditional legal solutions did not generally and *per se* wipe the idea of a factual consent of a child to sexual activities from the table. These people usually point to the fact that under the present laws, any such factual consent of a child to any child-adult sexual activity is deemed *legally invalid*. We face a tautology. The reply does *not answer* the question. It elegantly circumvents it.

Somehow, many researchers from the strata of more traditional-thinking people have in my view *not* totally excluded the possibility of a socially adequate range of non-violent sexual activities between children and adults, leaving open the possibility of a different and sexually more liberal social situation being one day realized *within a different legal system* that backs it up.

In the commentaries on *statutory rape* is to be found that the *factual consent of the child is legally invalid or immaterial.* This logically implies that such factual consent is possible! It is inconsistent, however, to continue arguing, as many traditional criminal law experts did and do, that children generally did *not know what they consent to* when it regards their sexual wishes or desires.

Children generally do have the ability to know what they find pleasurable and gratifying, on one hand, and what they find appalling, on the other.

Sexuality is a way of exchanging pleasure, it's a form of communication, and it is as such only one of various experiences that enrich our lives. And as with all other life experiences, there will be a first time when this pleasure is experienced and there will also be one or the other form of initiation into it. That such initiation of a child, when it comes from the side not of a child, but of an adult, should be abusive in every single case has little or no factual backup.

Research speaks rather for evaluating every case and restraining from general judgments because set opinions about the matter can hardly cope with the variety of possible experiences. More recent research has repeatedly confirmed that trauma is not generally experienced through the sexual initiation itself but through certain behavior from the side of the adult that the child feels is *inappropriate*, or that is *appalling* because of *coercion* or when the child is *silenced* by threat with the purpose of keeping the experience secret.

> —See Lauretta Bender & Abram Blau, The Reaction of Children to Sexual Relations with Adults, American J. Orthopsychiatry 7 (1937), 500-518, Brant & Tisza, The Sexually Misused Child, American J. Orthopsychiatry, 47(1)(1977) and M. Cook, M. & K. Howells (Eds.), Adult Sexual Interest in Children, Academic Press, London, 1980.

In commentaries on traditional sex laws it is often said that premature sexual knowledge and experience had to be avoided by all means or that early sexual experience would disturb the sexual development of the child. This argument evidently contradicts the truth that all in life grows and evolves according to experience and *not* according to avoiding experience; as such, this argument simply cannot serve as a basis for legislation. Upon deeper regard it appears to be an *ideological credo* that serves to maintain an artificial image of childhood that in little or no way cares about the true and actual needs of children.

It can be argued that in former highly patriarchal societies the much *greater power of an adult compared to the very low social status of a child* would invariably lead to abuse from the side of adults who sexually approach children.

There is certainly some truth in this, but the value of this argument changes considerably for our present-day culture that grants the child a much greater range of rights than those that have ever before existed in human history.

According to research, violence and power abuse in sexual encounters between adults and children rarely occurs and is rather the exception than the rule of such encounters. While traditional child rearing required from the child an almost total submission under the commands and the authority of the adults raising and educating them, in modern democratic society the child is not invariably and totally subjected to authority but granted a substantial amount of freedom and personality rights that include free speech and a still expanding range of options and freedoms for self-realization as well as a constantly growing impact upon deciding about his or her own professional future.

It can even be argued, and it is rhetoric among leftist groups in Western society, that it is this authoritarian system in politics, society and family itself that brought about *child abuse* in the first place, and not the modern view that considers children as members of the community in their own right.

It cannot be denied that physical child abuse was and is to a large extent justified by patriarchal morals; however, this matter is controversial regarding *sexual* abuse. Traditional circles of society tend to blind out the existence of child abuse or *project it on sexual minorities*; on the other hand, more progressive circles tend to overreact and exaggerate child abuse in modern society.

Whatever opinion one may personally have, it cannot be denied that our culture that is still basically patriarchal has built, over times, a high degree of *structural violence* that makes it very difficult to change sexual laws because of a basic lack of trust in the self-regulatory systems inherent in nature.

This is why only a responsible legislator can change those laws rather than waiting for a majority of the population to be ready for this change. Modern legislation must care about the best of the subjects to be protected by the law, as is children in this case, and not or much less about ideological, religious, traditional or custom opinions of the majority of the population.

Of course, in an authoritarian system children range among slaves and abuse will occur without being called abuse. In a democratic society, however, children are partners and have choices to engage in life in ways that may be unthinkable in highly controlled social systems, but that are going along with the child's need to grow, and also grow in autonomy.

There is no essential difference between the effects of physical and sexual violence against

THE LEGAL SPLIT IN CHILD PROTECTION

children. Both forms of violence can have traumatizing effects on the child's psyche. By contrast, in the absence of violence in sexual relations, children tend to receive some form of gratification from the experience. In addition, psychology has corroborated that children are *emotionally indiscriminating*, and that it is generally not the age of a possible partner or mate that is decisive for them to love this person, but other, emotional factors such as friendship, care, closeness, availability, understanding or continuity.

A study conducted by Sigmund Freud's daughter Anna Freud on children kept in shelters during the heavy German bomb attacks in London during World War II came to the result that children are not invariably emotionally attached to their parents but to anyone who cares for their nutrition and emotional needs.

> —Anna Freud & Linda Burlingham, War and Children, London: 1943.

As a matter of fact, some of the children only unwillingly accepted to get back to their parents after the end of the war because they had *emotionally attached to one or the other caretakers* in a shelter. The study also concluded that fear is nothing inherent in children, not even in war times but a result of the parent's own fear that is transmitted to them telepathically or by implicit action.

By themselves, and without parental enticement to be afraid, Anna Freud concluded, *children are rather matter-of-fact and able to enjoy virtually any situation that arises, how dangerous it ever may be.*

From all the factors that are decisive in sexual relations between children and adults, one factor has been found the *least* pertaining: *the child's age*. A girl of sixteen can be totally unable to consent to a sexual activity with a peer or an adult while a girl of four may feel safe and competent to agree to sex with an adult she loves. Sexual development in fact has shown to depend much more on factual and positive life experiences than on certain biological key events. The latter are still necessary and important to happen but relatively secondary with regard to a child's factual love capacity. The inherent dangers that also the present bill cannot deny, namely that children can become victims of emotional or sexual exploitation, are equally independent of the child's age.

These dangers exist *for all children*, with the difference however that the experienced child will be much more able to cope with unwanted sexual approaches than children that are raised in overprotection, fear and guilt and sexual ignorance. Highly protected children have shown to be much more vulnerable to exploitation than children who can experience love and sexuality according to their own curiosity and the opportunities that life brings to them naturally. Children raised in authoritarian settings are generally unable to cope with unexpected situations because in the normal course of events decisions are taken *for* them and not *by* them, and they are not the rulers of their destiny.

By contrast, children from more liberal families tend to develop a more or less effective self-protection that shields them against actual exploitation. The law does not have and does not want to have the function of keeping children immature but must consider children as beings-in-growth in accordance with the child's need to build more and more autonomy as they grow up. Effective legal protection can only be provided on the basis of equal rights of children, and it has to be seen that the abandonment of authoritarian structures in education will in last resort make the passive submission of children to physical or sexual attacks on them *less likely to occur.*

On the other hand, it is often argued by criminal lawyers that a legal system with strict ages of consent bears the advantage to provide strict guidelines about what is permitted by the law and what is illegal. There is certainly some truth in this argument. But apart from the fact that in love encounters it is quite uncommon to inquire about the exact age of a mate, I claim that for adults to assure that the sexual activity with a child they engage in is non-violent under the definition of a statute is a legal fact *easier to verify* than finding out about the exact age of a child.

A future legislation should be sex-affirming, positive and rational, as well as effective for defeating violence. It should not be moralizing, but built upon scientifically corroborated findings and experiences. As such its primary intention should be to prevent violent crime, and violent sexual crime, instead of nailing people with useless draconian punishments. To achieve this goal, the legislation should be highly restrictive toward violence encompassing even slight forms of psychic pressure under its definition.

Such an approach would then be consistent with the insight that it is violence that is to be feared, that is dangerous to a child, an adult or the community as a whole, and not sensual pleasure and sexual diversity. Basic novelties of such a future legal bill should be the *abandonment of any age of consent and the retreat of state and federal authorities* to ruling and policing into the family and into love and intimacy, thus abandoning the age-old persecution of nonviolent and consenting relationships between persons of different age, regardless of their sexual or non-sexual nature. Eventually, the most daring novelty is the *establishment and authorization of special consultants* to effectively deal with cases that represent violent physical or sexual attacks on children.

The allocation of the burden of proof should be drafted as an exception to a general rule of non-violence against children put up as a starting point of the bill. With regard to the criteria of the activity in question to be *non-violent*, it should be legally presumed that the child consented to the sexual activity when that activity was nonviolent and that the child was generally able to estimate to what they consented to, except in those particular circumstances where consent was deemed legally invalid.

In cases of doubt, the defendant should bear the risk that consultants prove that the child was unable to give consent either by showing that there was no factual willingness of the child or by proving that the child lacked the necessary ability to make an informed decision. The burden of proof should be reversed when the activity was to be qualified a violent sexual assault as an aggravating judicial circumstance.

Research demonstrated that physical violence against children cannot effectively be dealt with by a legal dichotomy of lawful *corporal punishment*, on one hand, and unlawful child battery, on the other.

Besides the fact that under some jurisdictions even brutal and truly harmful physical attacks on children would still be justified as lawful *corporal punishment*, if only the parent or educator acted *in good faith*, the dividing line between the two areas is extremely difficult to draw and the legal uncertainty thus considerable. This lack of sharpness of the pertaining laws is certainly not for the good of the child. It rather *serves the perpetuation of an authoritarian, repressive and inhuman educational system* that is outdated because it produces uncreative, fearful, and co-dependent human beings. And whatever position one may take, there is no doubt that both corporal punishment and child battery are violence inflicted upon children. From this argument, it appears clear that there is no rational reason to treat both forms of behavior in a different way. Actually, the only difference is an internal factor—*good faith*—which is what lawyers call a *chewing-gum clause* because it's very hard to prove or disprove in reality and thus serves judge and jury to get at about any thinkable outcome that serves to corroborate their *feelings* and that, by doing so, opens the door to all and every form of prejudice.

The intention of any democratic and childcaring legislator can only be to prohibit the infliction of violence upon children.

Moreover, it has no rational basis to give certain adults such as parents or educators a free license to physically attack a child for whatever reason, educational or other.

The general law policy behind the future legislation on prohibiting violence against children should consider that mere gifts or promises given in exchange to sexual favors *are not depriving the child of their personal autonomy* and do not directly impinge upon the child's psyche. In general, they can be said to represent, to a certain extent, socially adequate behavior in that they are not directly, but only indirectly impacting upon the child's consent.

In the same way as a child can accept or refuse kisses and caresses already as a baby, they can accept or deny to engage in any nonviolent sexual activity, and this regardless of age. The burden of proof should be with consultants for the fact that, in the particular case, the child did not consent to the sexual activity when *prima facie* such consent was given.

It is equally on the consultants to prove that the child exceptionally lacked the capacity to estimate what they consented to. If the defendant did not know about the child's state of incapacity to consent, the consent of the child should legally be deemed to be valid. Such a provision is important for those rather exceptional cases where the child was *willing and consenting* but mentally retarded without appearing to be retarded, or in any other way in a state of mental or emotional confusion or incapacity to

THE LEGAL SPLIT IN CHILD PROTECTION

consent, while however *appearing* to be normal. It should be presumed by the statute that children do not consent to violent physical or sexual interactions. In order to rebut this presumption, the burden of proof should be on the defendant for the fact that, beyond reasonable doubt, the child consented to the activity despite its violent character.

To summarize, what I suggest as a drafting technique for any future bill that sets out to unify the social fight against physical and sexual violence against children, commonly called *physical and sexual abuse*, is to follow the principles of drafting statutes established for civil law procedures, as they are valid, still today, not only in the United States and the United Kingdom, but also in former members of the British Commonwealth called *common law jurisdictions* such as, for example, Canada, Australia, New Zealand, South Africa, India, Pakistan, Burma, Singapore or Sri Lanka.

Such an approach would be in accordance with my initial proposal to decriminalize sexual behavior for all members of society, and establish a consulting service composed of *trained and experienced psychological, psychiatric and sexological advisors* to deal with these matters as legally empowered professionals working for the public good and in execution of governmental duties and responsibilities.

Chapter Three

Child Protection Draft Bill

§1 Preliminaries

(1) The state government of any state having adopted the current bill, and the federal government restrain from interfering in sexual behavior among consenting people whatever their age. This rule is to be referred to as 'general rule of non-interference.'

(2) The state government of any state having adopted the current bill, and the federal government restrain from interfering in matters involving the physical punishment of children and all related issues.

(3) For all matters under this bill, competent *pedoemotions consultants* act as *entrusted representatives* for all state and federal administrations.

THE LEGAL SPLIT IN CHILD PROTECTION

Commentary

The bill starts with a general rule of non-interference that is the turning point that this new legislative draft offers, as it provides a new paradigm for child protection.

The bill provides a *pleasure-affirming, positive, functional and rational* approach to defeating violence that was drafted after long consideration of the pleasure-violence dichotomy proven scientifically by the research of *Herbert James Campbell* and *James W. Prescott,* and research on the pleasure function and love conducted by *Ashley Montagu, Michel Odent* and others. The solution taken was to free all love-related behavior out of the hands of the state administration, recognizing that intimacy of consenting people whatever their age oscillates within the very core of fundamental human rights, and can thus not be *criminal* by definition.

An essential trigger to the change was the insight that sex laws, when they were drafted in the past, were not motivated by human rights considerations, but in the contrary by a desire of religious and worldly institutions to *control and regulate human behavior* without any regard of the fundamental right of any human to live a free life, and intimacy, when no aggression is done to others or the state. In addition, these laws were founded upon moralism and fear.

The statute is not built upon vague and unclear moralistic considerations, but upon scientifically corroborated findings and experiences, and as such intends to *prevent crime instead of nailing people with useless draconian punishments* for having mishandled their *emotional flow*. In fact, the draft bill bans violence in every form, encompassing even slight forms of psychic pressure under its definition.

This approach is consistent with the insight that it is violence that is to be feared, that is dangerous to a child, an adult or the community as a whole, and not sensual and sexual pleasure and sexual diversity.

§2 Competencies of Consultants

(1) For all matters under this statute, the principle of state retaliation against, or punishment of, an individual that offends the law was replaced with *Pedoemotions Consultancy (PEC)*. Matters involving love, sex and the family cannot be properly handled by police and criminal authorities, but if ever by specialists who possess *adequate psychological, sociological, biological and sexological knowledge.*

(2) For all matters under this bill, *pedoemotions consultants*, here thereafter called 'consultants,' are empowered to handle these matters in accordance with applicable laws and regulations.

The Ministry of Education, in coordination with the Ministry of Justice, sets up nationwide regional study and course centers for *Pedoemotions Consultancy (PEC)*.

(3) The decisions of consultants regarding matters under this bill are binding for all state and federal authorities and for all parties involved.

Their overall purpose of operation is to bring about effective, peaceful and beneficial solutions for all matters under this bill, and for all parties concerned.

Commentary

> Basic novelties of the bill are the abolishment of age-of-consent laws and the retreat of state and federal authorities from regulating human love and intimacy, thus putting an end to the age-old persecution of nonviolent and consenting relationships between persons of different age, regardless of their sexual or nonsexual nature. Eventually, the most daring novelty is perhaps the establishment and authorization of special consultants to effectively deal with cases that represent violent physical or sexual attacks on children under §5 of the statute.

§3 Measures taken by Consultants

(1) In no case under this bill shall an individual be detained, forced, punished, fined or degraded

because of his or her actions falling under sections 5 to 8 of this statute.

> COMMENTARY
>
> PEC is not intended to humiliate, punish or discipline citizens who have badly handled their emotional flow or pedoemotions. Its purpose is to prevent crime, and to understand the true reasons of crime before crime is committed.

(2) All measures to be taken by consultants are exempt from law enforcement as provided by police or prosecution authorities, and criminal justice at large.

> COMMENTARY
>
> This paragraph was inserted to prevent law enforcement to get hold of citizens who would enjoy the protection of the present bill by attacking consultants, and here especially by declaring certain measures taken in certain cases as illegal. They may do so, but only by filing a formal complaint to the competent federal and state authorities who regulate the professional ethics of consultants, not by directly interfering in pending consultancy cases, using their administrative powers. To allow them such interference would jeopardize the applicability of the present bill.

(3) Measures to be taken by consultants range from one month to two years of consultancy for

individuals who have violently assaulted a child as defined in §5 of this statute.

(4) Measures to be taken by consultants range from one year to five years of consultancy for individuals who have violently assaulted a child as defined in §5 of this statute and where lasting irreversible trauma or lasting irreversible physical or psychic harm was caused to the child as a direct result of the assault.

(5) Measures of appropriate healing and care are to be taken for children involved in cases of violent physical or sexual assault on a child under §5 of this statute.

(6) The examination and investigation, by consultants, of a child subject to a violent physical or sexual attack under §5 of this statute has to be accomplished without any influence or moral pressure upon the child's judgment.

(7) Physical or sexological/gynecological examination of a child is not indicated in cases where the degree of violence was minor as defined in §5(2) of this bill, and has generally to be proportional to the gravity of the harm done to the child.

Commentary

§§(3) to (7) of this section find their rationale in the different intensity of harm done to a child under sections 5 to 8 of the bill; consultancy measures have to be proportional in scope and strength to the gravity of the harm done to the child. In alignment with this general rule, sub-section (7) contains a rule of non-interference or restraint in a case where the degree of harm done to a child was minor according to the definition provided by §5(2) of the bill.

The gynecological examination of a girl child's vagina or anus, or the examination of a boy's anus is *more than a minor intervention* into the body of a child. Tools and tubes are used to open the sphincter of the child to see if the integrity of the skin has been severed by any forced penetration; in this sense, *the examination by itself is a minor form of penetration and does a certain amount of harm*, which is certainly not justified to be done to a child in a case where only minor harm was done in the first place. Under the old sex laws, children were regularly examined that way even in the case where it was clear from the start that the sexual behavior in question was only of a fondling and caressing nature without an even slight attempt of penetration.

In such cases, there is an obvious misbalance between the actual harm done to the child and the harm done by the intervention of law enforcement. Such a legal situation cannot be upheld as it is against the very foundations of criminal law, namely the principles of *adequacy and proportionality* of the state's response to any harm done to a citizen; as such, the situation under the old sex laws was largely unconstitutional.

§4 Definitions

(1) Consent and Willingness

(a) Willingness is the actual willingness of a child for participating in any activity. Consent is the voluntary expression, verbally or otherwise, of this willingness.

Commentary

This sub-section distinguishes between consent and willingness of a child. Former sex laws did not make this distinction that has been largely accepted by the literature. In fact, those old laws declared any consent or willingness of a child to any sexual activity as legally invalid. It appears that under those antiquated laws, the child was considered not as a person, but as an automaton without feelings, without a personal will, and without a decision power, when only sexual behavior is concerned.

The discrimination between nonsexual and sexual behavior when considering a child's expression of their will to participate in a shared activity or not, is irrational and logically not sound. It only makes sense under a legal situation that protects not the child, but a principle of 'public morality' or however one calls it.

This very detail in how the old sex laws handled the child's *actual consent or willingness* to a sexual activity with an adult shows that these laws were not targeting to protect children from harm; they were rather targeting at protecting society from sex.

As such, these laws were neither rational nor natural, but simply life-denying and fundamentalist in the worst sense of the term. And it is for this reason that they were ineffective in their overall purpose on protecting the child from any real harm done by sexual violence. In fact, as long as these laws were in place, and criminal sentences steadily were scaled up even for minor sexual play with a child, statistics showed a yearly increase in violent nonsexual and sexual assault on children. This went as far as jailing for many years a father who had tickled the vagina of his girl child, which is really where law punishes life, by punishing emotionally and sensually nurturant parents. It's a case where laws were historically on a borderline to insanity.

Such laws could therefore not responsibly be upheld under the present doctrine of *rational, effective, reasonable and proportional lawmaking*.

(b) The initiative, taken by a child, to engage in a sexual activity with an adult is legally deemed as the expression of the child's consent to this activity.

THE LEGAL SPLIT IN CHILD PROTECTION

COMMENTARY

This sub-section puts an end to the long-discussed question if so-called 'seductive' or 'sexually provocative' children have to get a special treatment in child protection. Under the old legal situation, they were not given a special treatment, and even worse, they were treated as delinquents and often put in special care. It goes without saying that punishing a child for being sexual is against all logic and life's inherent purpose of childhood being of a temporary nature. A child who is premature in whatever field, be it sex, piano playing (there are 4-year old concert pianists over the while course of musical history!), physics, sports, chess, video gaming or any other area, should be rewarded, and not punished. As Françoise Dolto put it in *Psychanalyse et Pédiatrie (1971)*, a child who is sexually premature and is often found masturbating is a child who should be given more freedom, *more responsibility* and access to higher academia. Herself was an example; she read *professional medicine textbooks* at the age of five, and at that early age already signaled to her parents that later she wanted to become a 'child doctor.'

(2) Burden of Proof

The burden is on consultants to prove that in case of a nonviolent and non-harmful sexual activity between an adult and the child, the child was not willing to agree with sex and did not express any form of consent to it.

Commentary

The allocation of the burden of proof is drafted in line with the general rule established in §5(1). With regard to the criteria of the activity to be nonviolent according to §6(5), it is legally presumed that the child consented to the sexual activity when the activity was nonviolent and did no harm to the child, and when the child was generally able to estimate to what he or she consented to, except in particular circumstances where consent is deemed legally invalid.

In cases of doubt, the burden is thus upon consultants for proving that the child was unable to give consent either by showing that there was no factual willingness or by proving that the child lacked the necessary ability to make an informed decision.

The burden of proof is reversed when the activity was to be qualified a violent sexual assault under §5 of the bill.

§5 Violence against Children

(1) No parent, person in loco parentis, educator or other person responsible for the care of a child has the right to corporally punish a child. Violence against a child, whatever the motives are for inflicting violence, is considered to be *child battery*, also in the case that the battery was done with the intention to discipline the child, except in the case that the degree of the violence was minor as defined in §6(2).

(2) 'Violence' in the sense of subsection (1) means a physical, psychic or sexual attack on a child that causes the child to experience physical pain or psychic stress. This is particularly, but not exclusively, the case when the attack causes lasting physical or psychic harm to the child. A *sexual attack* on the body of the child requires penetration into the body of the child, with a sexual organ or any tool, causing pain to the child, and which is intended to either bring about sexual or nonsexual gratification without the child's consent, or enforce the child's compliance or submission to a certain behavior, or which is intended to reprimand the child for unwanted behavior.

(3) A 'physical or psychic attack on a child' in the sense of subsection (2) encompasses also the detention of the child, the deprivation of food, the physical abandonment or neglect of the child and other cruel treatment that presents an immediate danger to the safety of the child.

(4) 'Corporal punishment' in the sense of subsection (1) is violence against a child that is intended, by causing pain, to bring about the child's compliance, or the child's submission to certain

behavior, or which is intended to reprimand the child for unwanted behavior.

Commentary

Research has demonstrated that physical violence against children cannot effectively be dealt with by a legal dichotomy of *lawful corporal punishment*, on one hand, and *unlawful child battery*, on the other. Besides the fact that under some jurisdictions even brutal and truly harmful physical attacks on children would still be justified as lawful corporal punishment, if only the parent or educator acted 'in good faith', the dividing line between the two areas is extremely difficult to draw and the legal uncertainty thus considerable.

This lack of sharpness of the former laws was certainly not for the good of the child. It rather served the perpetuation of an authoritarian, repressive and inhuman educational system that produced uncreative, fearful and co-dependent humans. Whatever position one may take, there is no doubt that both corporal punishment and child battery are violence inflicted upon children.

From this argument, it appears clear that there is no rationale in treating both forms of behavior in a different way. Actually, the only difference is an internal factor—good faith—which is what lawyers call a chewing-gum clause because it's very hard to prove or disprove in reality and thus serves judge and jury to get at about any thinkable outcome that serves to corroborate their feelings and that, by

THE LEGAL SPLIT IN CHILD PROTECTION

doing so, opens the door to all and every expression of prejudice.

The intention of a democratic and childcaring legislator can only be to prohibit the *infliction of violence* upon children. Moreover, it has no rational basis to give certain adults such as parents or educators a free license to physically attack children for whatever reason, educational or other.

Regarding *sexual violence* against children, the bill had to be explicit in discarding any consenting behaviors and any behaviors where the child is fondled, caressed, kissed, stroked, or where shared nudity is experienced or where child and adult were naked co-sleeping or taking baths together, or where the sexual activity consists in *mere 'outercourse'*, that is, the adult restricting himself or herself to rub their body against the body of the child to reach an orgasm.

These behaviors cannot qualify as 'sexual violence' in the sense of the bill because their overall gestalt is one of caregiving in the larger ecstatic and pleasure-sharing sense. Under the old legal situation, it was namely rampant to see adults jailed for sensuality with children where the overall gestalt of the behavior is affectionate and caregiving with the difference only that the adult derives so much pleasure from giving care and love to the child that they come off sexually. However, such behavior needs to be encouraged, not punished, because it is the very pleasure function that maintains life, and that makes that adults care for children at all. Hence the bill's exclusive focus upon penetration in the body of the child as a *prime indicator for violence*, but here the definition 'sexual violence' would also only apply when the child's consent was clearly missing.

Under the old legal situation, intercourse with a child was per se considered as sexual violence, as the consent of the child was deemed legally valid. Such lawmaking overlooks however that intercourse is not always painful or disagreeable for a child when the partner is an adult and that it should be the child, not society or the state to decide for their love life, and hence, children should be able to say 'I want to experience this' or 'I do not want to experience this'. It is the child who is the target of protection, hence it must be the child to decide how much 'protection' from life and pleasure they need and how much protection they do not wish to experience. Research has namely shown since about the 1930s that violence is the foremost indicator for child trauma, not the nature of the sexual relation experienced, or the fact that penetration was experienced by the child.

§6 Consent

(1) The child cannot consent to physical or sexual violence, except the degree of violence was minor.

(2) The degree of the physical or sexual attack on the body of the child was minor if no physical pain or

psychic stress was experienced and no lasting physical or psychic harm was caused.

(3) Consensual intercourse between an adult and a child is not considered to be a 'sexual attack on the body of the child'. This also applies when the intercourse caused minor or short-lasting pain to the child and the child, despite the pain, did not expressly and visibly defend the activity.

(4) Consensual intercourse between an adult and a child is to be considered a 'sexual attack on the body of the child' if significant and lasting physical or psychic harm was caused by the activity and the child did not consent to the activity. Consent is lacking when the child first agreed to the activity, but then changed their mind, while the adult continued the intercourse until orgasm thus disregarding the child's decision to stop the activity. Consent is also lacking in the case that the child experienced either short-lasting but excruciating pain, or long-lasting pain, through the activity and was not listened to when signaling to stop the activity so that the intercourse was accomplished until the orgasm of the adult partner.

(5) Temporary abrasions in the genital or anal region or soreness of the vagina or anus are not to be considered as physical harm.

(6) Tearing of the hymen of a girl-child by vaginal penetration and intercourse is to be considered as lasting physical harm under the terms of subsection (4), except the child expressly consented to her losing the hymen during the intercourse. The burden of proof for the child's consent is upon the defendant.

(7) In any case under this paragraph of the statute, when an adult stops the intercourse on the demand of the child, especially, but not only, when the child expressed the will to stop the activity because of experiencing pain, the burden of proof is reversed and consent of the child is deemed to be valid for the activity until the point it was stopped. It is then upon consultants to prove that, exceptionally, the child was not giving a valid consent for the entire activity. If the latter is the case, and lacking consent being proved beyond reasonable doubt, the activity is to be considered a violent assault on a child under §5(1) of the statute.

(8) Lasting physical or mental injury of the child is to be admitted in the case that the child needs to

receive constant, and not only temporary medical or psychic health care and attention. This is particularly, but not only, the case when the child is confided to a mental health institution or if the child needs permanent supervision and medical care over the span of at least five subsequent years.

This is also, but not only, the case when an internal organ of the child has been so severely damaged during the intercourse, and as a direct result of the intercourse, that the organ is not functional anymore for the lifetime of the child without proceeding to an organ transplantation.

(9) Consent to a nonviolent sexual activity with an adult can be given by a child without regard to the child's age.

(10) The factual consent of the child is legally valid.

(11) *Prima facie*, the actual willingness of the child to sexual activity with the adult is deemed to be valid consent to the activity, except the contrary is proved. The burden of proof for the fact that willingness of the child was no valid consent is upon consultants.

(12) The actual willingness of the child to the sexual activity is *not legally valid consent* in the case

that the child could not estimate what they consented to. This is namely, but not exclusively, the case when the child was made drunk, was hypnotized or was given narcotics to induce willingness to sex or if their consent was forced by psychic pressure in the form of threat, but not if the child was merely enticed to the sexual activity by gifts or promises.

> COMMENTARY
>
> The law policy behind this provision is that mere gifts or promises given in exchange to sexual favors are not depriving the child of their personal autonomy and do not directly impinge upon the child's psyche and decision-making power. In general, they can be said to represent, to a certain extent, socially adequate behavior in that they are not directly, but only indirectly, impacting upon the child's consent.
>
> However, the same is not true for cases where the child was manipulated in any way, in order to influence their decision ability, typically through using hypnosis or substances to alter the child's mental state. In such a case, no consent of the child can be presumed.

(13) The low age of a child is no argument to invalidate factual willingness for a sexual activity.

> COMMENTARY
>
> In the same way as a child can accept or refuse kisses and caresses already as a baby, they can

accept or deny to engage in any nonviolent sexual activity, and this regardless of age.

However, the same is not to be assumed when the activity was violent in any way. It cannot be presumed by a reasonable lawmaker that human beings consent to being treated in a violent manner.

(14) The *burden of proof* is on consultants for the fact that, in the particular case, the child did not consent to the sexual activity when *prima facie* such consent was given. It is equally on consultants to prove that the child exceptionally lacked the capacity to estimate what they consented to. If the defendant did not know about the child's state of incapacity to consent, the factual consent is deemed to be legally valid.

Commentary

This provision is drafted for those exceptional cases where the child was willing and consenting but mentally retarded without appearing to be retarded, or in any other way in a state of mental or emotional confusion or incapacity to consent, while however appearing to be normal.

§7 Degree of Violence & Burden of Proof

Consent to a violent sexual activity is only legally valid if the degree of violence was minor as defined under §6(2) of the statute.

Commentary

It is presumed that children do not consent to violent physical or sexual interactions. In order to rebut this presumption, the burden of proof is on the defendant for the fact that, beyond reasonable doubt, the child consented to the activity despite its violent character.

§8 Family & Educational Relations

(1) A child can consent to a sexual activity with his or her parent, person in loco parentis, brother, sister or other relative, except in the case that the sexual activity was violent. Consent to a violent sexual activity is only legally valid if the degree of violence was minor as defined under §6(2) supra.

Commentary

The long-standing debate about incest is a rhetoric that is strongly tinted by moralism and life-denial. All serious and matter-of-fact research concludes on the harmless nature of incest when it is based on mutual

THE LEGAL SPLIT IN CHILD PROTECTION

consent, absence of violence and when the child is not emotionally entangled by co-dependence with one of the parents. It's the *emotional entanglement* that is *really incestuous* because it traps the child in a web of invisible strings that hold the child a captive of the matrix, the home, the family tree, and the family karma.

The *sexual part* of incest is the more harmless part of it. Historically, incest was equally forbidden between adults belonging to the same family or clan, which shows that the incest taboo had originally nothing to do with child protection or pedosexuality in the modern sense.

Another rationale of incest was historically the strong and dominant role of the father under patriarchy, which was a power position that could easily be abused. But research showed that the only way to counter such a dominant position of the father, with all the potential abuse that it entails, is to modernize society in a way that maximizes the equality between the sexes. Today, in industrialized countries and with urban population, the male cannot be said to have a very dominant position in relation to the female, and the child.

That is why, if society is at all serious about the original rationale of the incest taboo as a means of *preventing abuse,* incest should be monitored with equal emphasis in the mother-son relation; but the latter is not the case. Modern society is highly suspicious with regard to the father-daughter relation, which led to an almost complete segregation of fathers in child care, but it considers

114

mothers as potentially harmless while they often today entangle their (male) children in unhealthy co-dependence, thereby retarding their emotional and sexual growth.

The way out of this unhealthy fusionary entanglement in the modern nuclear family is a liberation of incest from its stigma which only creates guilt, fear and actually favors co-dependence, and to leave it up to parents and children to *acknowledge their possible mutual erotic attractions*, and at the same time provide children, through permissive laws, healthy love options outside of the family.

When people have real love options outside of the family, incest loses its attraction. It has been said with good reason that incest is a strange choice because one defended love partner is preferred over thousands if not millions of potential other love partners. Love and sex have to be learnt like anything else in life, and a responsible society organizes social life for all members of society, as this is the only really effective prevention of incest.

The bill thus considers incest as a phenomenon that is rather effect than cause and that is not naturally a viable love option, but becomes one because of isolation, sex prohibitions and insufficient love options outside of the family. For that matter, however, it is not to be considered criminal behavior but needs to be understood in each and every single case, and with applying not a 'police mindset' but emotional and erotic intelligence.

(2) A child can consent to a sexual activity with his or her teacher or any other person in charge for the child's education, except in the case that the sexual activity was violent. Consent to a violent sexual activity is only legally valid if the degree of violence was minor as defined under §6(2) supra.

COMMENTARY

Under the old paradigm, from about the end of the Hellenic and Roman empires and the beginning of Christianity, teachers were punished with particular harshness for any erotic relations with children in their care.

While in ancient traditions, erotic relations between teachers and students, habitually of a homosexual nature, were tolerated and considered, within the educated strata, as inevitable and harmless, modern society *castrated the teacher*, transforming him or her into an ascetic educational robot who 'spits out' knowledge on demand. At the same time, the quality of educational institutions was watered down and lost its soul and the important imbeddedness of all knowledge within a greater cultural setting that integrates all our emotions and desires and humanizes them through loving dialogue.

Education became lifeless and mechanical, and the teacher-student relationship formalized, rigid, and emotionally numb. While the official rhetoric was hostile to any, even the slightest, erotic overtones in the teacher-student relation, psychoanalysis was outright positive and affirmative as to the beneficial effects of love relations between children and their teachers. Françoise Dolto, the late French child therapist said in one of her workshops on child analysis that adolescents constitute themselves primarily through their *erotic homosexual transfer on their teachers*, and it was through this homosexual love transfer on some of their teachers they fall in love with that they complete their psychosexual development and develop true genitality. This was so, she explained, because while identifying psychosexually with each of their parents and developing the basis of their sexuality, this development was completed only in the relation with teachers in its genital dimension because 'only with them the child can bring about a fruit within a relationship of culture and knowledge.'

—Françoise Dolto, Séminaire de Psychanalyse d'Enfants, Tome 1 (1982), p. 98. (Translation mine)

It is presumed that children do not consent to violent sexual activities. In order to rebut this presumption, the burden of proof is on the defendant for the fact that, beyond reasonable doubt, the child consented to the activity.

BIBLIOGRAPHY

Contextual Bibliography

Abrams, Jeremiah (Ed.)

Reclaiming the Inner Child
New York: Tarcher/Putnam, 1990

Alston, John P. / Tucker, Francis

The Myth of Sexual Permissiveness
The Journal of Sex Research, 9/1 (1973)

Appleton, Matthew

A Free Range Childhood
Self-Regulation at Summerhill School
Foundation for Educational Renewal, 2000

Ariès, Philippe

L'Enfant et la Famille sous l'Ancien Régime
Paris, Seuil, 1975

Centuries of Childhood
New York: Vintage Books, 1962

BACHOFEN, JOHANN JAKOB

GESAMMELTE WERKE, BAND 2
Das Mutterrecht
Basel: Benno Schwabe & Co, 1948
First published in 1861

BAGLEY, CHRISTOPHER

CHILD ABUSERS
Research and Treatment
New York: Universal Publishers, 2003

BARBAREE, HOWARD E. & MARSHALL, WILLIAM L. (EDS.)

THE JUVENILE SEX OFFENDER
Second Edition
New York: Guilford Press, 2008

BENDER LAURETTA & BLAU, ABRAM

THE REACTION OF CHILDREN TO SEXUAL RELATIONS WITH ADULTS
American J. Orthopsychiatry 7 (1937), 500-518

BERNARD, FRITS

PAEDOPHILIA
A Factual Report
Amsterdam: Enclave, 1985

BRANT & TISZA

THE SEXUALLY MISUSED CHILD
American J. Orthopsychiatry, 47(1)(1977)

BIBLIOGRAPHY

Brongersma, Edward

AGGRESSION AGAINST PEDOPHILES
7 International Journal of Law & Psychiatry 82 (1984)

LOVING BOYS (VOL.1 & VOL. 2)
Amsterdam, New York: Global Academic Publishers, 1987

Bullough & Bullough (Eds.)

HUMAN SEXUALITY
An Encyclopedia
New York: Garland Publishing, 1994

SIN, SICKNESS AND SANITY
A History of Sexual Attitudes
New York: New American Library, 1977

Burgess, Ann Wolbert

CHILD PORNOGRAPHY AND SEX RINGS
New York: Lexington Books, 1984

Buxton, Richard

THE COMPLETE WORLD OF GREEK MYTHOLOGY
London: Thames & Hudson, 2007

Cain, Chelsea & Moon Unit Zappa

WILD CHILD
New York: Seal Press (Feminist Publishing), 1999

CALDERONE & RAMEY

TALKING WITH YOUR CHILD ABOUT SEX
New York: Random House, 1982

CAMPBELL, HERBERT JAMES

THE PLEASURE AREAS
London: Eyre Methuen Ltd., 1973

CAMPBELL, JACQUELINE C.

ASSESSING DANGEROUSNESS
Violence by Sexual Offenders, Batterers and Child Abusers
New York: Sage Publications, 2004

CHAPLIN, CHARLES

MY AUTOBIOGRAPHY
New York: Plume, 1992
Originally published in 1964

CLARKE-STEWARD, S., FRIEDMAN, S. & KOCH, J.

CHILD DEVELOPMENT, A TOPICAL APPROACH
London: John Wiley, 1986

CONSTANTINE, LARRY L.

CHILDREN & SEX
New Findings, New Perspectives
Larry L. Constantine & Floyd M. Martinson (Eds.)
Boston: Little, Brown & Company, 1981

BIBLIOGRAPHY

TREASURES OF THE ISLAND
Children in Alternative Lifestyles
Beverly Hills: Sage Publications, 1976

WHERE ARE THE KIDS?
in: Libby & Whitehurst (ed.)
Marriage and Alternatives
Glenview: Scott Foresman, 1977

OPEN FAMILY
A Lifestyle for Kids and other People
26 FAMILY COORDINATOR 113-130 (1977)

COOK, M. & HOWELLS, K. (EDS.)

ADULT SEXUAL INTEREST IN CHILDREN
Academic Press, London, 1980

COVITZ, JOEL

EMOTIONAL CHILD ABUSE
The Family Curse
Boston: Sigo Press, 1986

CURRIER, RICHARD L.

JUVENILE SEXUALITY IN GLOBAL PERSPECTIVE
in : Children & Sex, New Findings, New Perspectives
Larry L. Constantine & Floyd M. Martinson (Eds.)
Boston: Little, Brown & Company, 1981

DEMAUSE, LLOYD

THE HISTORY OF CHILDHOOD
New York, 1974

FOUNDATIONS OF PSYCHOHISTORY
New York: Creative Roots, 1982

EDWARDES, A.

THE JEWEL OF THE LOTUS
New York, 1959

EISLER, RIANE

THE CHALICE AND THE BLADE
Our history, Our future
San Francisco: Harper & Row, 1995

SACRED PLEASURE: SEX, MYTH AND THE POLITICS OF THE BODY
New Paths to Power and Love
San Francisco: Harper & Row, 1996

ELLIS, HAVELOCK

SEXUAL INVERSION
New York: University Press of the Pacific, 2001
Originally published in 1897.

ELWIN, V.

THE MURIA AND THEIR GHOTUL
Bombay: Oxford University Press, 1947

ERIKSON, ERIK H.

CHILDHOOD AND SOCIETY
New York: Norton, 1993
First published in 1950

BIBLIOGRAPHY

Farson, Richard

BIRTHRIGHTS
A Bill of Rights for Children
Macmillan, New York, 1974

Finkelhor, David

SEXUALLY VICTIMIZED CHILDREN
New York: Free Press, 1981

Fortune, Mary M.

SEXUAL VIOLENCE
New York: Pilgrim Press, 1994

Foster/Freed

A BILL OF RIGHTS FOR CHILDREN
6 FAMILY LAW QUARTERLY 343 (1972)

Foucault, Michel

THE HISTORY OF SEXUALITY, VOL. I : THE WILL TO KNOWLEDGE
London: Penguin, 1998
First published in 1976

THE HISTORY OF SEXUALITY, VOL. II : THE USE OF PLEASURE
London: Penguin, 1998
First published in 1984

THE HISTORY OF SEXUALITY, VOL. III : THE CARE OF SELF
London: Penguin, 1998
First published in 1984

Freud, Anne

War and Children
London, 1943.

Freund, Kurt

Assessment of Pedophilia
in: Cook, M. and Howells, K. (eds.)
Adult Sexual Interest in Children
Academic Press, London, 1980

Fromm, Erich

The Anatomy of Human Destructiveness
New York: Owl Book, 1992
Originally published in 1973

Escape from Freedom
New York: Owl Books, 1994
Originally published in 1941

To Have or To Be
New York: Continuum International Publishing, 1996
Originally published in 1976

The Art of Loving
New York: HarperPerennial, 2000
Originally published in 1956

Geldard, Richard

Remembering Heraclitus
New York: Lindisfarne Books, 2000

BIBLIOGRAPHY

GIL, DAVID G.

SOCIETAL VIOLENCE AND VIOLENCE IN FAMILIES
in: David G. Gil, Child Abuse and Violence
New York: Ams Press, 1928

GOLDSTEIN, JEFFREY H.

AGGRESSION AND CRIMES OF VIOLENCE
New York, 1975

GORDON, ROSEMARY

PEDOPHILIA: NORMAL AND ABNORMAL
in: Kraemer, The Forbidden Love
London, 1976

GROTH, A. NICHOLAS

MEN WHO RAPE
The Psychology of the Offender
New York: Perseus Publishing, 1980

GUNN, JOHN

VIOLENCE
New York/Washington, 1973

HÉROARD, JEAN

JOURNAL DE JEAN HÉROARD SUR L'ENFANCE ET LA JEUNESSE DE LOUIS XIII
Paris: Soul/Barthélemy, 1868

HOWELLS, KEVIN

ADULT SEXUAL INTEREST IN CHILDREN
Considerations Relevant to Theories of Aetiology in:
Cook, M. and Howells, K. (eds.): Adult Sexual Interest in Children
Academic Press, London, 1980

HOOD, J.X.

SEXUAL CURIOSITIES OF LOVE, SEX AND MARRIAGE
A Survey of Sex Relations, Beliefs and Customs of Mankind in Different Countries and Ages
New York, 1951

JACKSON, STEVI

CHILDHOOD AND SEXUALITY
New York: Blackwell, 1982

JOHNSTON & DEISHER

CONTEMPORARY COMMUNAL CHILD REARING: A FIRST ANALYSIS
52 PEDIATRICS 319 (1973)

JONES, W.H.S., LITT, D.

PLINY NATURAL HISTORY
Cambridge, Mass.: Harvard University Press, 1980

KRAEMER

THE FORBIDDEN LOVE
London, 1976

BIBLIOGRAPHY

Krafft-Ebing, Richard von

Psychopathia Sexualis
New York: Bell Publishing, 1965
Originally published in 1886

Laud, Anne & Gilstrop, May

Violence in the Family
A Selected Bibliography on Child Abuse, Sexual Abuse of Children & Domestic Violence, June 1985, University of Georgia Libraries, Bibliographical Series, No. 32

Licht, Hans

Sexual Life in Ancient Greece
New York: AMS Press, 1995

Liedloff, Jean

Continuum Concept
In Search of Happiness Lost
New York: Perseus Books, 1986
First published in 1977

Locke, John

Some Thoughts Concerning Education
London, 1690
Reprinted in: The Works of John Locke, 1823
Vol. IX., pp. 6-205

LOWEN, ALEXANDER

DEPRESSION AND THE BODY
The Biological Basis of Faith and Reality
New York: Penguin, 1992

FEAR OF LIFE
New York: Bioenergetic Press, 2003

HONORING THE BODY
The Autobiography of Alexander Lowen
New York: Bioenergetic Press, 2004

JOY
The Surrender to the Body and to Life
New York: Penguin, 1995

LOVE AND ORGASM
New York: Macmillan, 1965

LOVE, SEX AND YOUR HEART
New York: Bioenergetics Press, 2004

NARCISSISM: DENIAL OF THE TRUE SELF
New York: Macmillan, Collier Books, 1983

PLEASURE: A CREATIVE APPROACH TO LIFE
New York: Bioenergetics Press, 2004
First published in 1970

THE LANGUAGE OF THE BODY
Physical Dynamics of Character Structure
New York: Bioenergetics Press, 2006

MALINOWSKI, BRONISLAW

CRIME UND CUSTOM IN SAVAGE SOCIETY
London: Kegan, 1926

BIBLIOGRAPHY

SEX AND REPRESSION IN SAVAGE SOCIETY
London: Kegan, 1927

THE SEXUAL LIFE OF SAVAGES IN NORTH WEST MELANESIA
New York: Halycon House, 1929

MANN, EDWARD W.

ORGONE, REICH & EROS
Wilhelm Reich's Theory of Life Energy
New York: Simon & Schuster (Touchstone), 1973

MARTINSON, FLOYD M.

SEXUAL KNOWLEDGE
Values and Behavior Patterns
St. Peter: Minn.: Gustavus Adolphus College, 1966

INFANT AND CHILD SEXUALITY
St. Peter: Minn.: Gustavus Adolphus College, 1973

THE QUALITY OF ADOLESCENT EXPERIENCES
St. Peter: Minn.: Gustavus Adolphus College, 1974

THE CHILD AND THE FAMILY
Calgary, Alberta: The University of Calgary, 1980

THE SEX EDUCATION OF YOUNG CHILDREN
in: Lorna Brown (Ed.), Sex Education in the Eighties
New York, London: Plenum Press, 1981, pp. 51 ff.

THE SEXUAL LIFE OF CHILDREN
New York: Bergin & Garvey, 1994

CHILDREN AND SEX, PART II: CHILDHOOD SEXUALITY
in: Bullough & Bullough, Human Sexuality (1994)
Pp. 111-116

Masters, R.E.L.

Forbidden Sexual Behavior and Morality
New York, 1962

Mead, Margaret

Sex and Temperament in Three Primitive Societies
New York, 1935

Miller, Alice

Four Your Own Good
Hidden Cruelty in Child-Rearing and the Roots of Violence
New York: Farrar, Straus & Giroux, 1983

Pictures of a Childhood
New York: Farrar, Straus & Giroux, 1986

The Drama of the Gifted Child
In Search for the True Self
translated by Ruth Ward
New York: Basic Books, 1996

Thou Shalt Not Be Aware
Society's Betrayal of the Child
New York: Noonday, 1998

The Political Consequences of Child Abuse
in: The Journal of Psychohistory 26, 2 (Fall 1998)

Moll, Albert

The Sexual Life of the Child
New York: Macmillan, 1912
First published in German as
Das Sexualleben des Kindes, 1909

MONTER, W. WILLIAM

WITCHCRAFT IN FRANCE AND SWITZERLAND
Ithaca & London: Cornell University Press, 1976

MONTAGU, ASHLEY

TOUCHING
The Human Significance of the Skin
New York: Harper & Row, 1978

MONTESSORI, MARIA

THE ABSORBENT MIND
Reprint Edition
New York: Buccaneer Books, 1995
First published in 1973

MOORE, THOMAS

CARE OF THE SOUL
A Guide for Cultivating Depth and Sacredness in Everyday Life
New York: Harper & Collins, 1994

MOSER, CHARLES ALLEN

DSM-IV-TR AND THE PARAPHILIAS: AN ARGUMENT FOR REMOVAL
With Peggy J. Kleinplatz
Journal of Psychology and Human Sexuality 17 (3/4), 91-109 (2005)

MURDOCK, G.

SOCIAL STRUCTURE
New York: Macmillan, 1960

NEILL, ALEXANDER SUTHERLAND

NEILL! NEILL! ORANGE-PEEL!
New York: Hart Publishing Co., 1972

SUMMERHILL
A Radical Approach to Child Rearing
New York: Hart Publishing, Reprint 1984
Originally published 1960

SUMMERHILL SCHOOL
A New View of Childhood
New York: St. Martin's Press
Reprint 1995

O'BRIAN, SHIRLEY

CHILD PORNOGRAPHY
2nd Edition
New York: Kendall/Hunt, 1992

PATRIDGE, BURGO

HISTORY OF ORGIES
New York, 1960.

PLUMMER, KENNETH

PEDOPHILIA
Constructing a Sociological Baseline
in: in: Cook, M. and Howells, K. (Eds.):
Adult Sexual Interest in Children
Academic Press, London, 1980, pp. 220 ff.

BIBLIOGRAPHY

PORTEOUS, HEDY S.

SEX AND IDENTITY
Your Child's Sexuality
Indianapolis: Bobbs-Merrill, 1972

PRESCOTT, JAMES W.

BODY PLEASURE AND THE ORIGINS OF VIOLENCE
Bulletin of the Atomic Scientists, 10-20 (1975)

DEPRIVATION OF PHYSICAL AFFECTION AS A PRIMARY PROCESS IN THE
DEVELOPMENT OF PHYSICAL VIOLENCE A COMPARATIVE AND CROSS-CULTURAL
PERSPECTIVE, IN: DAVID G. GIL, ED., CHILD ABUSE AND VIOLENCE
New York: Ams Press, 1979

PRITCHARD, COLIN

THE CHILD ABUSERS
New York: Open University Press, 2004

REICH, WILHELM

CHILDREN OF THE FUTURE
On the Prevention of Sexual Pathology
New York: Farrar, Straus & Giroux, 1983
First published in 1950

THE FUNCTION OF THE ORGASM (THE ORGONE, VOL. 1)
Orgone Institute Press, New York, 1942

THE INVASION OF COMPULSORY SEX MORALITY
New York: Farrar, Straus & Giroux, 1971
Originally published in 1932

THE SEXUAL REVOLUTION
©1945, 1962 by Mary Boyd Higgins as Director of the
Wilhelm Reich Infant Trust

RENAULD, MARY

THE PERSIAN BOY
New York: Bantam Books, 1972

ROSENBAUM, JULIUS

THE PLAGUE OF LUST
New York: Frederick Publications, 1955

ROSSMAN, PARKER

SEXUAL EXPERIENCES BETWEEN MEN AND BOYS
New York, 1976

ROTHSCHILD & WOLF

CHILDREN OF THE COUNTERCULTURE
New York: Garden City, 1976

RUSH, FLORENCE

THE BEST KEPT SECRET
Sexual Abuse of Children
New Jersey: Prentice Hall, 1980

SANDFORT, THEO

THE SEXUAL ASPECT OF PEDOPHILE RELATIONS
The Experience of Twenty-five Boys
Amsterdam: Pan/Spartacus, 1982

BIBLIOGRAPHY

SATINOVER, JEFFREY

HOMOSEXUALITY AND THE POLITICS OF TRUTH
New York: Baker Books, 1996

SCARRO, A.M., JR. (ED.)

MALE RAPE
New York: Ams Press, 1982

SINGER, JUNE

ANDROGYNY
New York: Doubleday Dell, 1976

STEKEL, WILHELM

AUTO-EROTICISM
A Psychiatric Study of Onanism and Neurosis
Republished, London: Paul Kegan, 2004

PATTERNS OF PSYCHOSEXUAL INFANTILISM
New York, 1959 (reprint edition)

SADISM AND MASOCHISM
New York: W.W. Norton & Co., 1953

SEX AND DREAMS
The Language of Dreams
Republished
New York: University Press of the Pacific, 2003

SYMONDS, JOHN ADDINGTON

A PROBLEM IN GREEK ETHICS
New York: M.S.G. House, 1971

Vanguard, Thorkil

PHALLÓS
A Symbol and its History in the Male World
New York: International Universities Press, 2001

Von Riezler, Sigmund

GESCHICHTE DER HEXENPROZESSE IN BAYERN
Stuttgart: Magnus Verlag, 1983

Ward, Elizabeth

FATHER-DAUGHTER RAPE
New York: Grove Press, 1985.

Yates, Alayne

SEX WITHOUT SHAME: ENCOURAGING THE CHILD'S HEALTHY SEXUAL DEVELOPMENT
New York, 1978
Republished Internet Edition

Zukav, Gary

THE DANCING WU LI MASTERS
An Overview of the New Physics
New York: HarperOne, 2001

Personal Notes

www.ingramcontent.com/pod-product-compliance
Lightning Source LLC
Chambersburg PA
CBHW031921240526
45464CB00021B/621